Sufficient Grace

Kurt Alan Yanik

About the Author

Kurt Yanik is just a simple guy who loves Jesus, his wife and his kids. He never won a Gold Medal, Academy Award, never invented anything nor has he ever performed in front of an audience at Carnegie Hall. He definitely cannot sing or play any instrument though he loves music. His main goal in life has been to be a good husband and a good father.

He has seen a lot of life in his years and felt God's calling to help others through this writing. He hopes that the reader sees themselves or someone they know in this book. So many people are in need of help and we can be a part of their healing. It takes patience and love and above all a selfless attitude.

Kurt does not want any glory, fame or riches for this book but wants all the glory to go to God.

Dedication

This book is dedicated to my mother and nana. As much as a human can they truly loved unconditionally. Etta Mae (mom) and Lavinia (nana) were very special people and influenced me to be kind, trustworthy and especially treat women with great respect. My morale compass was set by these special ladies. They fueled my desire to fight for what is right.

Every time I open a door for a lady I think of my mom. Physically, you have been gone for a long time but you both have permanently been in my heart.

Thank You Mom and Nana

Nana

Mom

Preface

It was a summer morning in the late 1970's, I arose early to get to an appointment that would take me through several towns in upper Fairfield County, Connecticut. At the time, I was home from college living in Ridgefield, CT with my father and stepmother. The ride from Ridgefield to nearby Newtown was a familiar ride of about thirty-five minutes up Route Seven and eventually connecting to Route Twenty-five right off Interstate Eighty-four. Since it was early on a Saturday, the traffic was light, and I would reach my destination much quicker than anticipated.

I took a slight detour to the neighboring town of Brookfield. This detour took me to multiple familiar spots including my old neighborhood where I lived for twelve years. The drive brought back joyous memories but also made me reflect on the pain and suffering that also occurred at that residence. When I reflect on those years, I still feel a sense of loss of opportunities especially in my high school years. Embarrassment, shame, and pain drove me into survival mode and crushed me as well as my happy go lucky spirit.

As I drove down Newtown's Main Street, I passed the historic flagpole which was, for some odd reason, positioned in the center of the Road. This quiet unassuming town would in later years' experience the tragedy known as the Sandy Hook Massacre. In December 2012 a troubled young man armed with a rifle and a large amount of ammunition went to the elementary school in town. When he was finished, 26 people were dead, 20 of them were innocent children. That horrific event shook the nation.

I reached the road where I would turn left and head up the hill. My destination was now in sight. The campus like setting was beautifully landscaped and there were multiple buildings set up for administration, housing and there was a central building set up for visitor access. It looked like a college campus, but it was not.

I parked my car and headed to the visitor building and signed in. The woman behind the desk then provided direction to my destination. I walked about a half mile down a dimly lit tunnel, I could hear every step I took. The echoes in that tunnel were eerie. As I drew closer, I did not know what to expect this was my first time here, but I knew it was not going to be pleasant.

Once there, I was buzzed into the secure area and I walked toward a familiar face, but this person was not the same. Gone were the bright blue eyes and beautiful smile I have known all my life; they were replaced by a person who was worn out by life and at the time not mentally stable. I was not greeted warmly but was given a nod of acknowledgement. I hugged her and then asked, *"How are you, Mom?"*.

I was nineteen years old and my mother, Etta Mae Yanik, was in Fairfield Hills Hospital, a psychiatric hospital. The most important and loving person in my life was a shadow of herself and I could do nothing to help her. She was very ill and unfortunately, she was never to recover. This was just one event in a series of tragedies my siblings and I endured in the decade of 1970's.

Paul, a disciple of Christ, in the verse below begs God to take away his pain and God responded in a way that only God can.   Though he does not heal Paul, he provides even greater comfort by assuring Paul that he is with him and God's power inside him is greater than any healing.

*Three times I pleaded with the Lord to take it away from me. 9 But he said to me, "**My grace is sufficient for you**, for my power is made perfect in weakness." Therefore, I will boast all the more gladly about my weaknesses, so that Christ's power may rest on me. 10 That is why, for Christ's sake, I delight in weaknesses, in insults, in hardships, in persecutions, in difficulties. For when I am weak, then I am strong. 2 Corinthians 12: 8-10*

In my life I have had setbacks, tragedies, pain but through it all God's grace was always sufficient. In my joys, triumphs, contentment and happiness, God's grace was always enough. I always had **Sufficient Grace.**

In the song, *Say Goodbye to Hollywood*, by Billy Joel, there is a line that states that life is a series of hellos and goodbyes. I do believe it is true, but I also believe life is a series of if- then statements with decision points and events in our lives that shapes our outcomes and the directions we take. We all have looked back at times, and thought- what would have happened in my life if I did this and not that? I think it is natural to reflect in this manner without feeling regretful but to understand the frailties of our lives on earth and how things can veer in a different direction by a slight alternative decision.

Recently, I started to reflect on events in my life. Some were in my control but as you will read in this book a lot of events were out of my control. I made some wise decisions and some decisions I wish I could take back, but through it all God was with me. A verse in the bible that is quoted frequently by Christians is Romans 8:28 and it can be repeated so often that it can become cliché minimizing God's love and power to work in all circumstances. Our savior can turn bad into good and good into better, all for his glory and our best interest.

Romans 8:28 states, *"And we know that in **all things** God works for the good of those who love him, who have been called according to his purpose." NIV* If you notice I highlighted **all things**, so does that mean my mistakes, my errors, my lack of judgment, decisions I made too rashly, too slowly or no decision at all. It said **all things** so I guess it must mean everything as God shapes us into the people, he wants us to be. All my mistakes, failures, trials, accomplishments and decisions God used to shape me for his good. Pretty Cool huh?

I am asking you, as the reader, to have an open mind and let the book take you where it may lead you. It is not written for any specific audience. I am a Christian, a follower of Jesus Christ and that will never change. I will discuss my Christian conversion because it is such a big part of my journey.

Family support

I told my story to my family recently, my wife Michelle, son Kyle and daughter Paige. Both kids are in their early twenties. My wife has known my story, but I've never before gone into great details. She said what she had was a high-level understanding and that I seemed detached from feelings when I told her about the major events of my life. Now she had a clear picture of all the events. The kids knew very little but enough to know that my family was broken, and some bad things happened. In fact, nobody had heard my whole story until then. Looking back, was I wise in not letting people in on my pain? Maybe I underestimated some people, and someone could have helped me navigate the pain, but I went into survival mode. While I was in that survival mode God still brought people in my life just at the right time to be a blessing. When I needed money or a car, he made the way for those items and many more. Looking back, I know it was my Lord and savior rooting for Kurt Yanik to make it and become his son.

After sharing the details with my family, I thought about how my story might help others and bring glory to Jesus, rather than to those circumstances. I spoke with a friend who has written multiple books and she encouraged me to write this book. In writing this book I am straight-forward. I am a New Englander, and we are just that way. It may seem I have grudges against people but honestly, I have let that go a long time ago. I do not have any voodoo dolls of my enemies in a closet.

In respect to my wife, Michelle, I have shared all these stories with her. I was in my thirties when we married so I did have other relationships and experiences before her. I was not a choir boy. I will discuss my wife further, but to say she is the best thing that ever happened to me would be a major understatement.

A greater understanding today of mental illness and suicide enables us to discuss these things that were once held as dark family secrets. The human brain is the central organ of our nervous system. It is a very complex organ. I will not pretend to understand the intricacies of the brain. My knowledge is basic, unscientific and simple. I do understand that this magnificent organ is susceptible to illness. In the past, brain illnesses were not regarded with the same care and compassion as an illness in any other organ such as the heart, kidney or eye.

For a period of time from 1994-2016, I would suffer bouts with depression, anxiety and panic attacks. In 2016 it got so bad I required hospitalization for a period of several weeks. All along that time there were signs of my disease but a lot of time I was able to cope with it and move on until finally I could not. I will share my personal perspective on the agony, pain and hopeless feeling later. I will also discuss the triumph and joy that I feel today. People who have these diseases do not want it, your child does not want to be anxious, your mother did not want Alzheimer's nor did your brother want to have bi-polar disorder. We live in an imperfect world surrounded by chaos and very unpleasant things. Today, because I suffered, I can reach out to those who suffer with compassion, hope, advice and love. Therapy can be useful, especially with people who have suffered and can really understand what a person goes through.

We are complex people with all kinds of emotions and feelings. What might make someone cry might make someone laugh. We even act with emotions that we ourselves do not totally understand why we are displaying them.

I will make some suggestions and make observations, but my real hope is that you will understand a bit more of who Jesus is and why following him is the best decision you will ever make. Through all my tragedy I never blamed God. It was ungodliness that led to the woes and suffering in my life.

We have all heard of the Serenity Prayer

*"God, grant me the **Serenity** to Accept the things I cannot change, Courage to change the things I can, and Wisdom to know the difference."*
Reinhold Niehbur

The prayer has been repeated over and over again and it covers a lot of ground, but to take it a step further we must acknowledge our dependence on God daily in all our circumstances. For sure God gives us abilities but it is through his blessing and love that we can face each day. Knowing that Jesus has my back and is not out to get me is such a peaceful feeling and for me it was a true struggle getting to that place. God understood and dealt with me on that level. Giving up control has never been my strong suit.

Prayer for Guidance

Lord, each day we face decisions and circumstances. We pray for wisdom and guidance through your Word. Teach us to hear your voice. When we face challenges that we would rather avoid give us the boldness and strength to persevere knowing that you are ever present. We trust in you alone.

Prayer for you

Lord thank you for letting me be a blessing to whoever reads this book and those who will let your everlasting love and joy enter their heart. I am truly thankful for this opportunity to take what was bad and turn it into good. Draw this reader and myself closer to you. Help us to always see that you have a purpose in their lives and that you understand the pain we encounter. You are always with us.

My Early Years

I was a happy-go-lucky kid and a bit of a schemer growing up in Fairfield County Connecticut. I was born in Stamford, moved to a part of town called Springdale, then to Darien and then to Brookfield. Brookfield is so small, often when you tell someone you are from Brookfield they don't know where it is. You have to add that it's a town next to Danbury. Most of my growing up years were spent in the town of Brookfield.

The Yanik family was based in Stamford, Connecticut. The Yaniks had been there for a while. All my immediate family members were born in Stamford which is a quick train ride to Manhattan, NY. I know there are still a lot of Yaniks in that area of the state which is a very affluent area of the country. We lived there but we were not at all a rich family.

In Springdale we lived near a strawberry patch and we kids used to pick strawberries and roast potatoes and apples under a pile of smoked leaves. Whoever thought it was a good idea to give elementary school kids matches wasn't thinking straight but we lit the leaves countless times. One time I took a bite of a baked apple not knowing a yellow jacket was on it. It stung the roof of my mouth and I went screaming home like a deranged maniac. It took about a dozen popsicles to comfort me.

Before moving to Brookfield, where I spent third grade through college, I have vivid memories about my time in Darien. Darien is and was then a very affluent town but because it was old money you really did not know who was rich and who wasn't. A true indication of that was after playing at a friend's house the chauffeur would give you a ride home.

In my neighborhood, everybody knew me I would shovel driveways, walk dogs, and make quick trips to the corner store. I would be paid in money, movie tickets, candy, lunches, etc. I was never home, I told my mother where I would be and that could have been at someone's house watching the Yankees, playing with friends or hanging with an elderly neighbor who just needed company. It was a fun time where I ruled over a three-block empire. Everyone knew who I was and I was a little entrepreneur.

I would walk to and from Hindley Elementary School every day and rush home making sure my empire was intact before settling down to watch Hanna-Barbara cartoons. I loved Huckleberry Hound, Top Cat, Snaggle Puss and so many other characters. The show was on WPIX in New York and was emceed by Chuck McCann who would do various impressions and introduce the cartoons. Poor Magilla Gorilla never found a permanent home. I still have so many fond memories of watching those cartoons. Bugs Bunny would come a bit later.

One day while walking home from school a cute girl in my class asked me to come over to her house. I happily accepted and we hung out together that afternoon. I guess I was there a while because dinner time rolled around, and her mother asked me if I could eat with them and I told her my mother was fine with it. However, I never told my mom where I would be, and she was at home freaking out because I never came home from school. She called the cops who were out looking for me. Finally, my friend's mother was contacted, and I was sent home. Mom was not pleased, in the least. I got quite a spanking that evening. My 2nd grade love life was put on hold at that point.

We always played in the woods in the neighborhood and we imitated the TV show Combat. Combat was a WWII show about a troop of soldiers given special assignments during the war. It came on ABC on Tuesday nights at 8 pm and all the neighborhood kids would watch it anticipating our next assignment out in the woods of Darien. Watching it, I soon figured out that the guest star for that week was a dead man. Since he was there for one episode, the guest star would always get into a tiff with Sergeant Saunders but see the errors of his ways and save the troop usually by throwing a grenade into the German machine gun nest but sacrificing his own life. The show was in black and white. As a 2nd grader I came to the conclusion that the USA won the war because, for whatever reason, the Germans would run out in broad daylight and get shot while our troops hid in bunkers. The show took some poetic license with the way the war went.

I was Sergeant Saunders of Dubois Street in Darien and my men fell into line. I even had them walk with several paces of space between each guy as we were on our mission and had to be ready for a German grenade being tossed or a landmine exploding. The mission had to be accomplished and nothing got in our way. My little brother wanted to join in, so I made him the medic and he did a great job patching up the wounded. It was an innocent and fun time that I fondly remember but it was to end soon.

I am the middle child in the family, my brother is the youngest and my sister is the oldest. I am very proud of my brother and sister. Considering all that they went through, they have both become great parents and have raised great kids with their spouses. My sister was an elementary school teacher in New Milford for many years. She positively impacted many young lives. I continue to meet former students who think fondly of her and add that they were impacted by her keen focus on reading. My brother has a huge heart. He always looks-out for the underdog. He interacts easily with people and has been successful in his career. Like all siblings, we have our disagreements, but we stick by each other. We may have it out, but we don't allow outsiders to bash our siblings. I am not going to discuss them much in the book because I will not take liberties with how they felt or saw the events that unfolded. This is my story and I am telling it truthfully and from my vantage point.

We may all recall major events from our childhood that affected our towns, our country or the world. Like most people my age, I vividly remember that November day in 2nd grade when my teacher Mrs. Jewel, who I adored, came running into the classroom crying uncontrollably. President Kennedy had been killed in Dallas that day and school was dismissed early.   For several days, we did not have school. As a kid, I wondered why my television shows were not on as it was wall to wall coverage of the assassination.   I saw the shooting of Lee Harvey Oswald by Jack Ruby, live as my mom watched the events nonstop. It was so surreal and left a big impression on my memory. That image still rings in my head today.

While in Darien, the family suffered two major losses. My maternal grandfather, Burton Trefry, died suddenly and my father lost his Executive job. Both were significant events in our family for obvious reasons. Both events also played a big part in later family situations. My grandfather died at age 50 of a blood clot that traveled from his leg to his heart, unexpectedly taking his life. He went by the nickname Pete, everyone called him that. I was too young to really know him well, but both of my parents have told me that I reminded them of him. My sister tells me I looked very much like him.

According to Great-Aunt Mary, (his sister), my grandfather Pete was solid as a rock and was a strong respected leader of the family and community. He was a self-made man who actually built the house in which we lived in Darien. I've heard often that he was a sweet and kind man who cared deeply for his family. If he had lived, I wonder if he could have been the strong male influence that we needed in the family. Maybe he would have stepped forward and dealt severely with my father's behavior.

Beside my nana, my Aunt Mary really became the matriarch of the family and she was the best. Mary lost two husbands tragically one to an onsite work accident and the other to cancer. So, when I knew her, she was on husband number three. She lived in Stamford and took in two of her girlfriends who lived with her as boarders. They were family, Aunt Mary, Aunt Kitty and Aunt Hattie hanging out watching their soap operas while smoking cigarettes and drinking their adult beverages. They never stopped smoking and they smoked Pall Malls with no filters, so I remember their voices being pretty rough.

Without fail each Christmas I would hang out with them for a bit and watch *It's a Wonderful Life* while Aunt Mary cooked in the other room. We had our own version of the Golden Girls right there in Stamford those were loving times. I really underestimated the value that Aunt Mary had in my life and my family's life. Later on, she would be the one who called me to tell me of the tragic death of my mother.

The second loss devastated my father and I think that he never really recovered from that job loss. He was a high-level executive at a company and was doing really well, he would travel to DC all the time and according to him he shared a helicopter ride with Bobby Kennedy. He was crushed with the loss of this job and had to take several jobs including waiting tables to make ends meet. My father lacked a great deal in being a father, but he did the basics for a period of time, we had a roof over our heads and food. He could have abandoned us then but, that would come while we were living in Brookfield.

I started third grade in Brookfield. We moved there as my dad took a job with Perkin Elmer, the company that would later build the optical components of the Hubble Space telescope. We never knew what he did there, it was top secret. He claimed to have had high security clearance and years after retirement he still would never reveal what he did. It came out later that they built spy satellites for the US government. I still do not know what he actually did there on a daily basis.

Regardless, he considered this job a step down from his previous job. His ego would not allow him to be happy and just be thankful. We had a nice new house in a brand-new neighborhood within walking distance to Lake Candlewood. We could be a family with a new beginning with the ability to have new adventures, but my father never bought into it. Instead, he was bitter and really became a loner.

Brookfield was an oasis for a kid my age in third grade. We lived in a neighborhood with plenty of woods a pond and access to a big man-made lake. With the newness of the homes all the families were new to the area, which was really exciting. We had so many families with kids my age it was so much fun. We were never in our houses we were always outside playing all kinds of games and sports. Back then all the homes were only about 1500 square feet and since we were never home, we didn't care. Today I am amazed that a family of four complains that they do not have enough room in 3500 square feet. Seriously?

One neighbor had the best field in front of their house, and we would play all kinds of sports and games there. My pack of friends were always at our house or we were at their house playing some imaginary game. We had acres upon acres of woods to play in and a pond where we went frogging or skating when the pond froze in the winter. Plus, we had Lake Candlewood where I loved to go fishing.

In elementary school I enjoyed some popularity, I was voted class president in 4th, 5th and 6th grades and did absolutely nothing. I guess I was a good politician since I was elected each year. Maybe they voted for me because I made them laugh. I still love to see others laugh and I just loved to laugh. My campaign slogan was *"Don't panic vote for Yanik"*. I think I also promised extra recess and cookies and milk at break time. I failed on my campaign promises.

My fifth-grade teacher, Mrs. Hoffman, called my mother one day. She said I was not in trouble but asked that I lighten up on the jokes. I liked that I could make Mrs. Hoffman laugh. In sixth grade, however, my standup routine would come to a halt because Mrs. George did not play. I can hear her voice now *"Mr. Yanik silly time is over"* and she meant it. You just did not mess with Mrs. George.

My time in junior high was pretty much the same. There was one constant, I was an excellent student. Mostly A's with an occasionally B and from an early age if my pitching career with the Yankees did not work out, I wanted to be a lawyer. Even today, I am fascinated by the legal profession. Though that dream was never realized I would have a decision point late in my life whether to pursue law school or go back to work.

My favorite Psalm: A Psalm of David.

The LORD is my shepherd; I lack nothing. He makes me lie down in green pastures, he leads me beside quiet waters, he refreshes my soul. He guides me along the right paths for his name's sake. Even **though I walk through the darkest valley***, I will fear no evil for you are with me; your rod and your staff, they comfort me. You prepare a table before me in the presence of my enemies. You anoint my head with oil; my cup overflows. Surely your goodness and love will follow me all the days of my life and I will dwell in the house of the Lord forever. Psalm 23 NIV*

In tenth grade my Latin teacher gave us an assignment to pick out our favorite poem, prose or short writing. I picked the 23rd Psalm which was written by King David who was said to really understand the heart of God. Ironically my teacher picked the same writing, I am not sure about his faith, but my family definitely was not religious. Though we did not go to church very much we still prayed for our meals and had a limited understanding of who Jesus was.

I always had a tremendous admiration for Jesus and never understood why he was mocked; his life was a curiosity to me. I never understood when my friends would speak ill of Christ, I would ask, "What did he do that was so bad?" This curiosity would lead me to pick up a Bible and actually read it. I loved to read, and the Bible was a best seller, so it made sense to read it. That was my introduction to understanding that Jesus is Lord.

Even for the non-believer this Psalm is written eloquently, and it sounds rather Shakespearean when presented in the King James version. Above all Jesus is Lord, he is always with me celebrating the good times and wiping away the tears when I am in pain. He guides my life and sets me on a path of living according to his will and to do and act right. He protects me and watches over me and we have established a covenant between us that no man can break. He blesses me with things that I need not necessarily what I want. He provides a home for me where I will be with him for eternity. Please if you are a non-believer take some time and read this Psalm. It offers a great deal; in fact, it is the best deal you will ever get. After reading Psalm 23 then move over to the other Gospels Matthew, Mark, Luke and John.

Even today the 23rd Psalm has an enormous impact on me.

Prayer for understanding the Gospel

Lord at this time we ask you for the ability to comprehend your Word. As we read scriptures, speak to our hearts and minds. Let your truth penetrate the walls that we have erected because of pain or ignorance. Let us discover something about your character each time we read and above all know that you want the best for us in all we do.

Dark Decade

In the Psalm above, you might take note of the phrase through the darkest valley. From 1970 to 1980, I went through a true valley of the shadow of death, it was just a horrible time in my life. These were the years that should have been the best times in a young life. The times that could set up your future. A time of figuring out who you were and who you wanted to be. Basically, that time of innocence was not in sight for me, I was in constant survival mode.

My high school, college and initial career years were a time of great anguish and pain and I confided in no one. In those ten years I witnessed the destruction of my family, my dad's adultery, my dad's continual lies, my dad walking out on his family, my dad leaving us in financial despair, my mom's mental illness, my mom's hospitalization in Fairfield Hills, my mom committing suicide, my nana dying of stage four bone cancer and finally my stepbrother's suicide.

Each of these events happened one after the other. We all have events that happen in our lives that we must deal with but all of these coming at me during this decade was never ending. I really began to believe that I was worthless and that I was not worthy of anything good ever happening to me. To go through crucial years of my life feeling this way plus the shame of the situation took its toll on my confidence, self-esteem and self-worth. If you knew me back then I was operating on about 25-40 percent Kurt. I had the talent, ability, drive and confidence to do so much better.

Up to that point, I was a very good student. I was an A student and I was a very confident if not a bit of a cocky kid. My colleges of choice were Yale University, Boston College or the University of Connecticut (UCONN), in that order. I definitely had the ability and drive but that all came crashing down in high school where the events above started. I attended Brookfield High School. Since it was a small town, everyone knew everyone and for the most part knew everyone's business. Hiding what was going on in my life was not an easy task but somehow nobody really knew. Looking back should I have trusted someone with my pain? Who do you trust with this baggage? I couldn't handle or understand it so how could I expect someone else to.

People can be cruel plus I loved my mother so much and she was such a great person, I did not want anybody to think badly of her. She deserved such a better fate for her life. To this day the values my mother taught me have been instrumental in my life. My mom chose kindness, love and respect as her behavior tools and everybody loved my mom. The practice of not speaking about my family situation was one I embraced throughout the decade and most of my life. It would come back to haunt me later in as the years passed on. I really needed a release of my pain and I had nowhere to turn.

Academics, my social life and athletic life all suffered immensely in high school. My grades went from A's to C's and B's, my dreams of going to a good college and pursuing law faded away.   I had a lot of friends and for the most part I was very well liked but my friends in my high school and college never knew the real me. I felt cheated that I was unable to give the best of me and also people did not see the best of me.

My high school class had its cliques, it seemed we had our defined pods like a caste system. There were definitely the haves and have nots so there was no unity or real spirit to this class. I remember one of my guidance counselors telling me our class was the most selfish class she had seen in her years at the school.

I was an enigma to people because I hung out with a diverse group. I looked at people and were interested in individuals. One minute I would be hanging out with a guy who adored Diana Ross the next minute I would be doing bong hits and drinking Boones Farm Apple wine behind the Spa on Candlewood Lake Road. Boy, that stuff was nasty. It was weird but it was also very fun getting to be a part of such a diverse group of people. I did not necessarily like Diana Ross but my friend liked her, his excitement was real and he was interesting.

One thing I found appalling was sick individuals who can sense when you are feeling down, they smell blood like a shark and try and go in for the kill. I took too much garbage from too many people at that time of life but honestly, they were just echoing how lousy I was already feeling about myself. My family life was such a mess and a disaster it was hard for me to be focused on just normal day to day activities.

I had a long fuse and I would put up with just so much and then I would explode, and it was not at all pleasant for the person who pushed me too far. It also was a shock for my friends when they saw that rare side of me but frustration and hurt just piled up on my shoulders.

At times, I would be in a zombie state and developed several nervous habits. I was very fidgety with my legs and was constantly in motion. I just could not stay still and relax. I was in perpetual motion but was very guarded when I interacted with my peers. I remember in my sophomore year a very popular girl who was in all my classes called me vain. I honestly had to look the word up in the dictionary because I had no clue what it meant. When I learned the definition, I was shocked that she thought of me that way. Maybe she was just trying to get a spark out of me but if she really thought that then she was way off. Maybe that is how I came off by trying to protect myself. I would only let people in just so far back then.

Because of family dynamics I did not get my driver's license until my senior year and still had no access to a car. During my senior year I met a girl that I liked spending time with and we got along great and had a cool connection. I always felt I was not good enough for her and some of my "so-called" friends drove-home that point to me. Later I found out they had ulterior motives for feeding me this info. I later found out that two of the girls, who told me that I was not good enough, actually liked me and wanted me to ask them out. I find that confusing.

The girl I liked drove a green Alfa Romero while I rode a 26-inch Schwinn bike with a bumper falling off the back. There was no room on the bike for dating plus I did not feel I was in her class. To her credit she never acted like she was better than me. It was all me, it was in my mind. When it was just the two of us together, we got along really well, but I never really asked her out or asked her if she liked me. My self-esteem and self-worth both were in the toilet, so I am sure I acted awkwardly at times. I just wanted a fair chance with her and with my damaged spirit that was never going to happen. We stayed connected for several years and the last time I saw her I was having a bad day with my dad and I acted irrationally and never saw her again.

Looking back, I am most disappointed with the teachers and administrators in my school. At no time did my teachers, coaches or guidance counselors ever reach out to me and ask what was wrong with me. They knew me all along and saw the drop in my grades, they witness the struggles my sister had, where were they? They just didn't seem to care one bit. What a waste of opportunity to be the stabilizing person in a kid's life. It was a major letdown and some of them even seemed to relish in my anguish. I wanted so bad to break my ruler over my geometry teachers head and I would not have felt any guilt if I did. She was way over the top and I think insane in her treatment of me in a subject I hate to this day.

I was good in sports and was never given a fair shot to make the teams at my school. I did not have an athletic body. In fact, I think I had the same build as my favorite Yankee, Thurman Munson. Unfortunately, I suffer with a weight problem that I just recently found out is due to a very low metabolism. It became worse as I got older especially after taking multiple types of medications. I know it sounds like an excuse but it is true, I was and still am not a big eater so you can imagine my frustration level.

Simply based on my physique, my coaches never took me seriously and really never gave me a fair chance. It would have been nice if someone who saw this would have stepped up and mentored me. I stopped trying out for the basketball team after my sophomore year I was never going to get a fair shake or have a coach work with me. So, I played in Catholic Youth Organization leagues and other leagues where the talent was so much better and had a lot of fun. With few exceptions, I would not go to high school sporting events it would be a waste of time plus it was tough to see the less talented kids and relatives of school board members make these teams over me.

I was pushed to my limit when I was cut from the baseball team in my senior year. The coach put kids on the team that honestly could not chew gum and walk at the same time. My long fuse had now exploded, I was really angry and I had every right to be. The coach tried to still be my buddy and I would have none of that. I really did not care if I got suspended, I let him have it verbally. Unfortunately, I used language that should have gotten me in serious trouble.

He knew he was wrong and instead of seeing the nice kid who he thought he could push around he experienced the fed-up kid who was pushed too far. He looked at me stunned and did not report me to the administration. My friends on the team knew of this injustice and said nothing. Not playing enabled me to pick up a job and I umpired more baseball games for the Brookfield Baseball Association (BBA). I have to say, I took some pleasure in seeing the school team have a lousy season.

My favorite job of all times was umpiring baseball games for the BBA. I did it for multiple years from high school and even into college. While other kids were making 2 bucks an hour. I was making 10 bucks a game for 2 hours of work. All the younger boys I umpired seemed to have sisters in my high school class and I would joke around with them. I had no clue back then, until a friend pointed out to me, that all the attention and questions I received from some of the mothers of those boys was actually their way of determining if I would be a possible suitor for their daughters.

My self-esteem would never let me believe that anyone would be interested in me. Umpiring was my thing and since I was behind the plate the catcher would hear all my wisecracks and jokes. The batters were included in my joking around as well. I was in my element and I was really good at it. Even today I hear from some of those guys and they tell me how much they enjoyed when I officiated their games back then.

One day, at lunch, a group of us boys were talking sports and the best athlete in our class told me he could beat me to 100 points even if he gave me 50 points in a game of one- on- one in basketball. That means if I score 50 points before he gets to 100, I win. A lot of the people at the table heard the conversation and sided with the athlete. Bets were made and I knew I was going to clean up. In fact, to get more money on the table I reduced the points that he gave me to 30 points. I knew I was going to cash in. This guy had been my good friend since third grade. He invited me to his house to take on this challenge. The bet between us was $50 and he never had a chance, I beat him without the points. It was not close. I got to 70 before he got to 50.

When he went to pay-up, I would not take the money. In fact, I never brought it up in school. In my opinion that is what friends do. I did not want to embarrass him. So, what if I was out the money. Sadly, he would not afford me the same grace later in college which abruptly ended our friendship.

During this time, my life at home was very rough, my parents fought nonstop and at times it got physical. Horrific things were said to each other as my parents fought. My mom was not perfect, but it was mostly my dad who was the main culprit. My mom had left him several times during the marriage and came back for the sake of the family. In retrospect I wish she left dad for good earlier in my life. My nana and her family would have been a great support and we would have been able to stabilize things.

On multiple occasions arguments took place because dad would not attend our school or sports events. I remember once my sister had a singing solo in the school concert. Dad and Mom argued for hours because my father was not going to attend this performance. I am not sure whether he decided to go or not but it was a major blow out. Dad would hurt my mom over and over again and it was all based on his selfishness.

I never understood how my mom and dad ever got together. I actually would ask them this question, *"How did you two ever get together?"* My mom thought of others while my dad was a narcissistic person. Mom had a lot of friends; my dad never had any friends. My mom was involved in our lives, dad avoided participating in our activities. My friends and neighbors knew my mom, my dad was not interested.

It seemed that my dad always wanted out of the family; he was a very bitter man who never took responsibility for his actions. The only joy I saw in him was on Monday night when he watched the TV, western *Gunsmoke*. He never did things with the family, he lived in our house and he might as well have been a boarder.

My father was a very talented man, an incredible artist, dancer, singer and the best ice skater I have ever seen. I remember his impressions of old-time actors like John Wayne, Jimmy Stewart and Walter Brennan. He had showbusiness in his blood. His father John was a prop man for various movies and television shows from the 1950s to 70s. John Yanik started as a stage manager in Stamford, CT, he worked with Houdini and Laurel and Hardy. Talking to him was fascinating. He worked on many Billy Wilder movies which included, *Some Like it Hot*. He also worked on movies like *The Odd Couple* with Jack Lemon and Walter Matthau.

My parents were both 1930's depression era babies. I guess that might have impacted my dad's behavior. His parents were not the most loving people and his father was always on the road so things were probably not easy for him. He just never, in my opinion, tried to be a better parent than what he was. He only focused on the negative and spent time in isolation from the family. Later in the marriage he was in the hospital for mental strain and used that as an excuse for abandoning his family. With all the talent my father had he never shared these gifts or encouraged his children's gifts to grow. He really saw us more as a hindrance to his goals than as precious offspring.

During my high school years Mom, started to show the mental stress that would lead to her breakdown. She was just not the same person and was getting worse each day. The one thing she cherished and was good at was being a mother and housewife. She could see that her life as she knew it was crumbling and she could not stop the eventual train wreck. Going through my teenage years without a mother in sound state of mind and an emotionally absent dad did not set me up for success.

I really no longer had parental influence starting at age fifteen. Parents should guide and protect their children. My sister, little brother and I lost the security of home at an early age. Lacking safeguards, a sense of belonging, love and warmth really changed my view of myself and the world.

It was difficult for me to watch her change. She was sick, mentally drained from years of abuse and disappointment. All she wanted was to have a family and raise her kids. Mom and I had a special bond. The loss of her dad must have been devastating to both mom and my nana but I do not recall them discussing it much. I loved watching old movies with my mom, watching her cook and seeing how well she treated my friends even when she was slipping away. She had at one time been featured in the Brookfield Journal, our local newspaper, for some of her recipes.

If you came to my house during this time, you would get the best from my mom. You coming to my house was a treat for my mom. My mom would be excited to see you and she would talk to you and was sincerely interested in you. Etta Mae Yanik, would give you the shirt off her back, sew you another shirt and feed you lunch while you waited for the new shirt to be done. My mom made my friends feel they were the most important person in that room. You left a better person knowing my mother. Even today people who knew my mom tell me what a great person she was.

It wasn't wise to, lie to my mother it was not pleasant if you got caught in a lie. However, she would back you to the hills if you told the truth. One time my brother was accused of beating-up a kid in the bathroom at school. He was going to get suspended for something he did not do because a bunch of kids lied about what happened. My brother told mom that he had nothing to do with it and she marched into the principal's office and refused to leave until the truth came out. My mom scared the daylights out of those kids who lied, and they confessed to the truth and took their punishment. I saw my mom in a different light through that event. She was the Sweet Assassin. You didn't mess with my mom.

My early connection with Jesus was when we were young, and we would go to church with my mother and nana. Every night my mom would tuck me into bed pray with me and we would sing Jesus Loves Me. We were not a religious family but that nightly ritual and praying prior to each meal definitely stood out. My mom was a classy person. She had nothing in material wealth, but she was so dignified.

One of the best memories with my mom was during the 1972 Olympics. During the games we started to follow a runner name David Wottle who was this skinny runner of the 800 meters event. He was just your normal kid from the Midwest who wore a baseball cap as he ran in every event. He really did not look like much of an athlete. He had this wild kick at the end of the 800 meters which meant he was always behind until midway through the last lap where he would turn it on and pass multiple runners to win. My mom did not follow sports but for some reason she became enamored with Mr. Wottle. It was just thrilling to watch him. In the final race for the gold medal, he passed three other runners in the last 100 meters to win the Gold. I remember my mom screaming for joy as he won the Gold.   Do yourself a favor search YOUTUBE for *1972 Olympics with David Wottle*. The race is truly amazing.

My mom lived in an innocent world where people were kind to each other and treated each other with respect. She was ill prepared for a bad marriage and it most definitely took its toll on her. She never understood meanness, rudeness, hatred or other means of poor behavior. These types of behaviors were so foreign to my mother and would have a prolonged impact on her.

I did not go to many of my friends' homes during high school and college. I couldn't bear to see their normal family lives while mine was in tatters. I did not really understand a stable or a loving home life it was so foreign to me. I really felt very uncomfortable watching a loving family. If a girl asked me over her house, I would make up some excuse, to not make it there. I imagined I would have to explain my life to my friends' parents, so I hid. On the other side, I hated being in my house during my high school and college years and I would just go for walks or ride my bike just to get away. Although uncomfortable visiting most homes, I spent a great deal of time at the home of my best friend Keith Milan. I am so grateful to have had that parachute. Surprisingly, I was comfortable in the Milan's stable home. It was my escape from the pain and tension.

I relied on three things to get me through those years. My sense of humor, music and regrettably, marijuana. I said I was going to be honest, so I have to include the fact that I smoked a lot of pot during these times. I am not proud of it but it is the truth. I also drank but really only had a taste for rye or whiskey a cold beer was ok now and then and I never liked wine. It was all for the purpose of escape. Luckily, I was too cheap or scared to get into harder drugs though I did experiment a bit with some harder drugs. Thank God, I did not develop a dependance on more addictive harder drugs. I strongly advise against using drugs or alcohol to numb pain.

One evening after dinner, my friend who was eating over needed a ride home. I was sixteen and did not have my driver's license. For some reason my mom decided to use the opportunity and turn that ride home for my friend into a driving lesson for me. Only one problem, I was stoned out of my mind. I backed out of the driveway perfectly but did not straighten the wheel and drove right up my neighbor's lawn. Luckily, I missed the flower bed. My mother went absolutely crazy and my friend in back seat was snickering as I stopped the car in my neighbor's front yard. My mother took the wheel and that was the end of driving lessons with mom. She never suspected I was stoned. I was pretty much a daily pot smoker through my senior year and my initial college years.

I loved music and I would spend hours listening to every type of it. A lot of times, my friend Keith and I would go to the band room in school, and into an inner rehearsal room, close the door, put on headphones and just get lost in music. Emerson Lake and Palmer, Yes, King Crimson, and Cat Stevens were played during our study hall and lunch breaks. I would go to all kinds of concerts especially when I lived in New Haven, I would wheel and deal concert tickets and just had a lot of fun. I saw the Who, David Bowie, the Rolling Stones, ELP, Yes and many more bands. I still love music and still go to concerts but taking my wife to see King Crimson recently was a little bit too much for her. King Crimson is an acquired taste and they were very, very loud.

My greatest distraction was my humor and my ability to see situations in a humorous way. I have been told I have an infectious laugh and can start people laughing and we forget what we are laughing about when we get going. I truly love to laugh and make someone smile; people are so much more attractive when you see joy on their faces. Today, I am still a goofball and love to laugh. As they say, laughter is the best medicine.

The song Tears of a Clown really told all you needed to know about how I felt in the dark decade. The lyrics were written by Smokey Robinson and music by Stevie Wonder. If you ever get the question who wrote the music to Tears of the Clown you now know and can win the trivia contest. I did not cry a lot in fact I only remember breaking down in tears twice in the decade and those times will be discussed later. I was sad, and I was hurting so bad, the song is about a clown happy during the day but sad in the evening because of lost love. I was not sad over lost love; I was so sad, lost and damaged in life. I had a good poker face so I could fool everyone except Mrs. Milan, my friend Keith's mom.   I wanted so badly for people to see the real me and what I had to offer as a person.

My self-esteem was at an all-time low. The confident Kurt was gone but I did not give up or want any pity or for anyone to think of me as a victim. I saw a light at the end of this. It was dim but as I survived each setback it would get brighter and brighter. That light was and still is my Lord and Savior Jesus Christ. Even through all the pain and struggles he still loved me and wanted the best for me and wanted me to truly know he had my back. Though I did not see him, he definitely saw me as his son.

Senior Year

Several times during my high school time I asked my parents if I could attend Immaculate High School in Danbury. Immaculate was a Catholic high school many of my friends attended that school. I knew the coaches and I know I would have gotten a fair chance to play multiple sports there. My friends at Immaculate urged me to enroll in their school and I was so excited at the possibility. I begged my parents to let me leave Brookfield High. I would have stayed back a year if I had to. I really wanted to get out of Brookfield High. My parents rejected the idea. We did not have money for a private school nor were we Catholic, was their response. I knew that half the student body was not Catholic. In addition, we were not a religious family so not being Catholic was not a strong argument. But, they were the parents.

I do have fond memories of my senior year at high school I got to know some good people and finally felt like I did belong. I would go to parties and people would invite me to hang out with them. Often, I felt like Sally Fields at the Oscars, *"you like me you really like me"*. I always thought wow if they liked the 40% me what if they could have seen me at little higher percentage. I do have a sneaky feeling they always liked me but with all my hurt I was too blind and damaged to see it. I was asked to the prom, but it was not my thing and I would have felt too awkward that night.

Overall, it was not high school so much as the situation my family had placed me in. Having no adult in my life to help mentor or direct me was a major blow to me and it set me back years. Mostly I missed out on getting to be that boy from Darien, I still think about it today, not in a bitter way but more in a wistful way. Today I am a very blessed man though sometimes I look back in sadness of what I missed out on during these years.

As I finally seemed to fit in, high school came to an end. I didn't care so much about high school itself it was my future and my family's future that was now in question. The loss of my college dreams really devastated to me. Yale, Boston College and even UCONN were now out of the question. My grades were not great. It hurt more as some of my friends went off to Boston College and UCONN. I honestly was not jealous of them; I know they worked hard. I was really mad and upset with myself. *"How did I let this happen,"* I wondered. I was very disappointed at this time in my life it was a crushing blow which led me to make some mistakes.

College Years

With my mom's demise and my dad's absence, I was on my own from age 15. There was a roof over my head but that was basically it. As things got worse the roles were now reversed, I had the role of caregiver to my mom and nana. It was a duty all the siblings had to share in. It just is not how things should be but there was no choice. Parents are intended to guide us through our decision-making processes especially when we are about to face the world a bit on our own. I had none of this and I made the mistake of going to a college in New Haven. Southern Connecticut State University is a fine school and I am not disparaging the institution it just was not a wise choice for me. Plus, I was needed at home and should have stayed home.

In hindsight, I should have gone to the local university in Danbury. I could have taken a few classes and worked. I was very close to doing that in fact I almost asked my friend if she could help get me a job in her father's factory. Being home might have helped my mom through an impossibly difficult stretch. Would it have made a difference? I do not know but looking back I wished I had given it a try.

I did not like dorm life it was so confining and was in an all-male dorm with a bunch of football players. The school was a commuter school and there was nothing to do for fun. What was the sense of going away to college if you were going home every weekend? Also, there were so many rules that I felt like prison more than school. I had more freedom during my high school years.

In New Haven, I realized how easily I interacted with African Americans. This may not be a big deal to most, but I came from a lily-white upbringing. The only people of color I knew were foreign exchange students in my high school. My new African American friends accepted and included me. I was even invited to a Sadie Hawkins dance by several nice young women. I know it sounds cliché, but I quickly realized people are people and I enjoyed and learned a lot from these friends. Racism and hatred had no place and would have no place in my life. Maybe God was preparing me early in life since my lovely wife is a Jamaican native.

I enjoyed the town of New Haven. Often, I would attend Yale University events and concerts at the old *New Haven Coliseum*. New Haven has the best pizza in the country, and it is always depicted on the Travel Channel or the Food Network. The New Haven Coliseum was the worst designed building ever. The arena was actually built below street level. You would park your car in a garage above the arena. The drive up to the parking deck was full of hair pin turns all the way to the open parking level. It's crazy, they let a bunch of stoned concert-goers drive up and down this maze. Not a great idea. It does not exist anymore and was destroyed by planned explosives in the mid 2000's.

The plan for attending Southern Connecticut State was to complete my time there in two years and transfer to UCONN. The University of Connecticut is a school in the northeastern part of the state, and it is in the middle of nowhere. After several attempts, I was finally accepted at UCONN and it was time to leave New Haven, the pizza, Yale and the Coliseum. I was to transfer shortly and was very excited about going to one of my original schools of choice.

Defining Moments

I came home one weekend while still attending Southern Connecticut State shortly before entering UCONN to study natural resources. That major seemed like a good idea at the time. In another era it might have been a good idea, but we were in the Carter administration and there were no jobs. Upon arriving home, I found my mother in the kitchen holding a piece of paper. It was a note from dad informing us that he had left the family. My dad took his clothes, a dresser and one of the cars. Leaving one car for my mom, my brother and me to share. My dad sneaked back into the house after pretending to go to work, when he knew no one was home, packed his things and took off. He wrote a pathetic note telling us he loved us, but he had to leave and did not tell us where he went. He left his family for his own selfishness and desires.

Dad had been planning his escape for a long time by hoarding money. I believe this because he left us flat broke. We never took vacations or spent money on any things for pleasure. He was stashing money for his escape and it made sense later on. When my mom died, there was no inheritance for us kids. We got absolutely nothing and I for one needed money for college and to survive since I was on my own. Prior to mom's death we had just sold the house in Brookfield so where was the money from that sale, how could it be kept from her, and from her kids?

Mom's reaction to the note was one of shock yet calm, she showed no emotion. I was stunned, but also calm. It was almost a relief. For weeks we didn't even care to know where he was. The next time I saw him was at work at the end of the semester. I took a summer job in the maintenance department at Perkin Elmer where he worked. It was a brief encounter; I don't even remember if he said anything to me.

The real story is he was having an affair, found another family and executed his escape plan. When I did ask him where he was, he made up a story that he was staying with some friends. I know he lied because my dad never had any friends. One day I was driving in town and saw him drive pass me, there was a suit jacket hanging in the back of his car. I decided to follow and went as far as Ridgefield. I finally decided to stop following him. I really didn't want to know where he was going. I know he was heading to see his girlfriend whom he later married. They married within a year of him leaving mom. Mom was already starting to crack before he left, and she soon would have to be hospitalized in Fairfield Hills. I had to finish the semester but would come home every weekend to see her.

My dad lied about everything and I mean everything. I truly think he lived in his fantasy world and actually believed his lies. He would lie about the silliest things that really did not have any relevance. It was always done to make him sound like he was a such a big, important man. Even in his senior years, he lied about friends, going to the doctors, going to church, where he planned to be buried, his adultery, pretty much everything. After a while some of the stories were so ludicrous that you just shook your head when he opened his mouth.

After dad left the house, my nana called me and asked that I come to Stamford one weekend to drive her back to our house in Brookfield. She was worried about my mom and she was lonely, so it was best that she lived with us. At this time my nana was getting frail and we just assumed it was old age. We did not know that she would soon be diagnosed with Stage 4 bone cancer.

I needed to get our car, so I needed a ride home from New Haven. I asked my friend from high school for a ride. This was the same guy I beat in the basketball challenge and refused to take his money. He agreed to give me a ride. I met him at the house he shared with another guy from Brookfield. I got along with this guy, but I always thought of him as a spoiled person who had a boat, lake house and a brand-new Camaro. He would brag about all his girlfriends in high school, but the elephant man could have gotten dates with all his toys. What irked me the most was his cruelty towards me during that time. Remember the people I talked about who will kick you when you are down? He was the king of that jungle and like a fool I took it. When I got to the house to meet my friend for the ride home, I thought we were leaving right away but the other guy was making a roast beef dinner for his housemates. He threw a fit that I was there and without talking to my face shouted from the kitchen that he (meaning me) would not get any food. I was really angry, but I needed to get home and had only one option.

I sat on the couch steaming, waiting for my ride as they ate in the next room. My nana is dying, my mom is sick and this child is pulling this stunt. I'd had enough! If I didn't need a ride so badly, I would have shoved that roast up... well, you get the idea. Plus, it was raining that night and I needed to focus on getting to my nana and getting her home. Something shifted inside me. I vowed from that day to never take any more junk from him or anybody. I was done being a patsy. I have not spoken to this person since that time. I honestly hope he has grown up and developed some class. I do forgive him, but I do not like what he did. Overall though I thank God for this event it toughened me up and I dealt with people on better terms.

On the drive home my friend asked me what was wrong because I was not talking to him. He knew what was wrong, he knew he was wrong for not having my back through this and other events with that guy. I felt betrayed by my friend, but he was a weak person who would not take a stand for his loyal friend. I thanked him for the ride and ended what I thought, up to that time, was a great friendship.

Later on, in the late-nineties I ran into him at a deli near Newtown. I was returning from an IBM business trip to NYC, I stopped there in route to my home in Farmington Ct, to call my wife and get something to drink. The deli is a quick stop off the highway and I would routinely stop there on my trips to New York. We talked for a bit, but he did not look good and he was a shell of the person I knew and liked all those years ago. My heart actually ached for him; he was a good person, but life seemed to have gotten the better of him. He died soon after that meeting, he was way too young to pass way.

> *Then Peter came up and said to him, "Lord, how often shall my brother sin against me, and I forgive him? As many as seven times?" Jesus said to him, "I do not say to you seven times, but seventy times seven." Matthew 18:21-22*

Though I was a poster boy for a person who could have been angry bitter and resentful I could not do it. Even before I became a Christian I had to move on and forgive people. I am not one to hold grudges and I could never hate. I got that from my mom. Mom just could not understand why anyone could be cruel or mean it was not rational to her and that hurt was part of her downfall. She expected kindness in return for kindness, I became a bit more jaded and a lot less trusting.

In the scripture above Peter, a disciple, ask Jesus basically how long should I put up with someone's nonsense. Peter was a hot head and was expecting Jesus to come up with an exact number. By Jesus saying 70 times seven, really meant there is no set number just be forgiving. That's what Jesus does for us when we fail by sinning, he is there to pick us up and put us back in the game. He loves us unconditionally and the power of forgiveness is so intense.

Prayer for Forgiveness

Lord, please forgive me of my sins and show me where I have not forgiven another. Reveal any anger, bitterness or unforgiveness so that I can deal with it now. Make me a person who is quick to forgive and quick to seek forgiveness. Thank you for the gift of forgiveness and the ability to move forward with our lives.

Fairfield Hills

The story is about to enter the darkest part of the dark decade. Remember these events were for the most part sequential. Everyone in my hometown and surrounding areas was aware of Fairfield Hills Hospital and what it was, a psychiatric hospital. At that time psychiatric facilities were referred to by multiple insensitive terms. You wouldn't want anyone to know you or someone you loved had been there. As I mentioned before, Fairfield Hills was in a neighboring town, Newtown. The hospital on a picturesque hill housed patients and medical staff in a campus like setting. It sat on over 100 acres of land.

Mom was getting worse; she would not sleep and when I was home, she would wake me up in the middle of the night pacing in my room. She was worried about everything, money, the bills, selling of the house, cooking, baking, the laundry. Some of it was reasonable but not at three in the morning. Each day she was getting worse and worse and it got so bad she was talking gibberish.

She was also pretty mean during this time. That definitely was not like her, this made me really suspect that something was seriously wrong with her. It was unlike her to be demeaning, rude, irritable or angry. Also, it did not help my siblings' nor my self-esteem.

While finishing up my last weeks of school in New Haven my mother was committed to Fairfield Hills. She would be in and out of Fairfield Hills several times over the next year before her eventual suicide. I am nineteen years old my dad is gone; my nana is dying, and my mother is in Fairfield Hills. Not your ideal situation, all during this time I was very aware of my situation and my surroundings as I watched other kids my age having a lot less to deal with. Boy did I crave just one normal day to not have all these burdens to deal with. I pushed through each day knowing better days were ahead and I was adamant, there would be nobody pitying me or looking at me like I was a victim. I could have benefitted from some compassion though.

After mom died people would ask me if I miss my mom. I missed my mom while she was still alive, since I was fifteen years old. Watching her slip away was crushing and she was never the same person. Being a caregiver for mother and nana was so draining. I was in a fog most of the time instead of progressing in my life everything seemed to move in slow motion and my life took a backseat. I still showed my poker face and would not tell anyone about my dilemma. I was in extreme survival mode which meant in my case withdrawing from my friends. Who would possibly understand this, who could I trust, who would care about the things I had to deal with? The answer is only Jesus could get me through this time and he constantly open doors for me at the perfect time.

Some of you have seen a loved one fade from you because of a mental disease. Today, Alzheimer's and Dementia are horrible diseases and some of you have seen family members who have suffered. They looked the same, but they do not remember anything or don't even know who you are. Eventually they will need to have special care and they must leave their home. You feel helpless as basically you are watching them die and act in a way that is disturbing and so unlike the way you want to remember them. I totally know how you feel, and you have my utmost sympathy. You want to remember them as they were, but it is difficult.

The worst part of the Dark Decade was visiting mom at Fairfield Hills. It was just horrible driving up the hill and parking my car and walking to the building where family were escorted to the patients. As I described before, Fairfield Hills had tunnels underground where you could walk to the various buildings in the overall complex. That was a dark cold walk which was at least a ½ mile away, it seemed like forever to get there. I felt like I was in one of those underground caverns that are depicted in a lot of World War II movies. The utter despair and hopelessness I felt walking down that corridor is something I find impossible to really explain. Gloom and doom were evident in each step I took with such a sense of sadness and horror as I was going to see my mother in a place, she did not deserve to be in. It was the last place I wanted to be, but I loved my mom and I needed to be there.

Once there you were let into an area that reminded me of a movie that came out around that time called, *One flew over the Cuckoo's Nest*. It was surreal that mom was in this group and they had her so doped up she could barely stay awake. You have to understand, this was my mom, the kindest person in my life was a virtual vegetable who had the limited ability to truly communicate.

On one visit I took my brother along with me. Looking at his face was probably a mirror reflection of my facial expression. The horror, the sadness and feeling of loss was all over his face. I know it truly freaked him out as well it should have. It drained us of all emotion and drained us physically. After a visit there you were just spent.

My job at the time was to protect my younger brother, he had less time with mom in her right mind than any of us. I really tried my best to keep him from some of the painful activities, but it was impossible because things never stopped happening. He deserved better; we all did. I had a lot of bad days but that was the worst day of my life. I had no hope that mom would ever get better and I was unfortunately accurate in my assessment. The darkness, the absence of good or any joy was constantly upon me and my family. Even when you did the right thing it would not change anything. You just survive day by day.

Each trip to Fairfield Hills was more gut wrenching and daunting as the prior one. It was a horrible experience that got worse on each trip. I would not allow my nana to visit mom there, it would have just been way too much. Fairfield Hills has since closed and the land has been used in various ways over the years. Since my last visit, I have not gone back to that area.

Signs of Mental Illness

I am not a therapist, doctor or a psychiatrist but I have been around enough mental illness to understand some of the signs that a person might display while struggling with mental illness.

- Isolation from others is a sign that something might be amiss. The person can either isolate physically or mentally, I did both. I remember being in a crowd of friends but still feeling all alone and not engaged. I could fake it by nodding my head without knowing at all what is being said.
- When nothing is good, everyone is annoying, the slightest situation sets a person off, that is a sign that a person is not coping well with life. The agitated response to the simplest situation can indicate a problem
- Feeling of hopelessness even when things are going really well or finding fault with everything. Hope keeps us alive. I love the New York Giants and I used to joke with my wife that I loved the Giants more than her but I loved her more than the Yankees. I was kidding. I got so depressed that I would not even care if the Giants were playing that day. I was so out of it, luckily, I was fine during their four super bowl wins.

- Thoughts and imaginings. Sometimes it is paranoia, fear, thinking about one thing or topic over and over, or a troubling imagination that leads to panic attacks. Panic attacks can cause physical sensations in the body, like changes in body temperature. Unpredictable swings from feeling very hot to very cold sometimes occur.

Of course, anxiety is the most recognizable of the symptoms of mental illness. Some people are very anxious but not necessarily ill. Anxiety in itself is bad not just mentally but can really affect your health and can cause a lot of sicknesses. Strains to our mental state has proven to have a major effect on our physical wellbeing.

If you see a loved one with any of these symptoms get them help and do it with love and without any judgment. Help them with love and with caution and do not give up, trust me they need you. Patience is needed in support of people affected with mental issues. People just do not snap out of it they will need time.

One of the things that did help me with my anxiety and depression was exercise. I ran and played all kinds of sports and was active nonstop. As I got older and more settled the lack of intense exercise plus other factors made me susceptible to illness. Staying busy and intense exercise are not the only answers to fixing the illness because there will be a time when you slow down and the issues will hit you like a train. That is exactly what happened to me. I just burned myself out working crazy hours, incredible work stress and ignoring some of my signs. Please do not ignore signs in yourself or any loved one.

It is not easy to confront people who are suffering but we all must try to help our loved ones. It will be challenging but through prayer you can be such an asset in someone's life and be a part of their healing.

Medications

I could write a whole book on medication. I will say that in my opinion, the medical community has gotten way too prescription happy. I have been on so many different types of medications and I would say overall it was a lot more harmful than good. The side effects like weight gain, sweating, insomnia and dry mouth are a few I encountered and there are many more side effects.

Some of these medications are potent, one of my medications was listed as addictive and I had to spend time detoxing off of this drug. Trust me that was not a fun process at all especially while I was struggling with my illness. It seemed to me that I was a human guinea pig to these doctors.

Just look what has happened with pain killers like OxyContin and others that are highly addictive but are prescribed for legitimate pain and result in addiction which leads to illegal use. So many lives lost for basic greed.

I am not advising against using drugs because they can be effective. My mistake was that I put way too much trust in the medical community and did not do my homework. Most physicians I ran into are very limited in skills when it comes to mental issues. Research every medicine that you take and find a good medical team even if you have to pay extra for it. The upfront effort will save you a lot of time, money and it will give us a better chance at success.

UCONN

What should have been a joyous time finally going to UCONN was now becoming a decision point. Do I go to school or stay home and help out around the house? My sister had moved back, and my brother went to live with another family to complete his high school years. Our family home would soon be up for sale and my dad moved back in for a bit to get the house ready for sale. I decided to go to school and it was the right decision for me. Being around my father at that time would not have been a good thing for me.

Driving up to UCONN that day I was still worried about my decision. I went up with my friend Keith and he knew most of what was going on. He noticed that I was very fidgety that day. He later said that I was not just fidgety I was physically shaking. I was leaving my family behind but starting a new adventure. Since I was a transfer student, I was put in temporary housing until other dorm space became available. I wish I could have stayed there; we were a group of students in the same situation. We were like vagabonds that no one wanted. I became friends with a lot of those vagabonds which carried on through my time at UCONN.

I became close to one girl in particular while living in temporary housing. Her first and last names rhymed. Like myself she was born in Stamford, CT and her dad was a camera man for the New York Yankees. For that reason alone, I should have kept the relationship moving. We just spent a lot of time together and we did simple things together like walk, browse record stores and just talk. I really liked her. She was the type of girl who did not draw attention to herself even though she would be the prettiest girl in the room. She was perfect for me; she did not do drugs or drink. I on the other hand was abusing those substances at this time. Her goal was to join the Peace Corp after she left school.

We should have had a longer relationship throughout our time there. Her influence on me was nothing but positive, she was not high maintenance and she was just happy with the simplest things. I really respected that she did not do drugs and alcohol and I was totally fine with that. Three months into our time together my mom took her life and I became a zombie and did not think anything good could ever happen to me. So, I let this innocent and sweet relationship fade away. She was a big fan of the singer Robert Palmer and when I hear one of his songs on the radio, I sometimes think of her. She was a blessing to me during a tough time in my life, but I did not want to burden her any further with my damaged life.

This was a pattern I would repeat with a lot of my dating relationships. As I stated before I was well aware of my situation, if I got too close to any girl I dated, the subject of my background would eventually come up. Telling anyone about my family demons was something I wanted to avoid. So, I just didn't meet girls' parents or go to their homes. Any good parent would want to know who their daughter was dating and to know my background. What would I tell them my dad is an adulterer, my mom is in a mental hospital and there is mental illness in my family? Not a winning formula. In that day and time, any parent would be leery of my past and my current dilemmas and I would not have blamed them. A good parent protects their children and though you can say it was not my fault, it was my baggage.

I did not know who to trust so I trusted no one with my background. I missed out on some really great relationships and it is why almost all my relationships started out as friends and grew into other things. I was never a big boyfriend-girlfriend person, I figured if you like hanging out with someone and it turned into something else you have both a friend and a mate. I knew my wife for several years before we dated.

Overall, I loved UCONN. The school used to be an agricultural school so it was a beautiful campus with sprawling acres and hills. At this time, I took up running it really helped calm the anxiety and sadness I was dealing with. I was like Forrest Gump; I would run all around the campus and in the woods and some of my woman friends became my running partner. Unlike Forrest Gump there was no Jenny and I did not have people following me. I looked forward to my run every day, it was a soothing form of energy release.

While at UCONN. I was broke. My roommate was a guy from Greece. He was the best roommate ever. He worked at Willington Pizza which was close to campus. He told me they needed a delivery man and I took the job. So, every Thursday, Friday, Saturday and Sunday I worked from 6 p.m. to around 2 a.m. delivering pizza. I got a buck per pizza delivered and up to ten bucks if there was a big order like ROTC deliveries. There was down time so I would meet with friends or girlfriends during the shift. College kids did not tip in money so I would get a beer, joints or bong hits for my services. I was pretty buzzed most of the time, delivering pizzas.

The owners of the pizza joint were Greek immigrants. They had two cute little girls who I entertained between my deliveries. They both loved Shaun Cassidy so I teased them a lot about that. They treated me like I was part of the family. I could help myself to food and drinks whenever I wanted. I even took the wife out dancing a couple of times. She was a lot younger than her husband. We talked as we closed the shop together each night. I do not know if he just trusted me or if it was that he didn't care. Regardless, I never betrayed his trust in me with his wife. She was a friend and that alone. Overall, they made me feel special. There was a biker bar next door. They cut a window between the two businesses so we could slide food to the hungry bar patrons. The bikers could not have been more friendly and kind to me and my Greek family. We were a diverse group having a beer together, a group of bikers, Greek immigrants and me from Brookfield, CT.

My Greek family was so good to me and I was invited to their house for the holidays. I remember one Christmas I went to their house and they surprised me with multiple gifts. We drank ouzo and we did Greek dances with the kids. I worked with them for a year and a half and they sold the business and moved to another town in Connecticut to open a family-style restaurant. That was a blessing in my life that I fondly remember. It allowed me to see that there was some good in people.

I loved UCONN and knew I had to make decisions about my future. Keith and I settled into our major, Natural Resources. It sounded good and I think I would have loved maybe working in a National Park, as a park ranger since I loved the outdoors. One evening I went with a bunch of my resources friend to hear a pitch from a current employee of the park services. As he talked, I began to have second thoughts about this major. Due to government cuts getting a job was a virtual impossibility and even if you got a job the pay was terrible. I would make more delivering pizzas for a living. That night my band of friends and I got very drunk and closed down the university pub. We had no future, we thought.

I also attended forest fighting training for a few days. This job is absolutely insane I do not understand how these guys do it. First the equipment you wear is like one hundred pounds. I was sweating and there was no fire in site plus you stopped the fire by digging ditches around the fire. The theory is the ditches will stop the spread of the fire, good luck with that. The final shock was watching firefighters parachute into the fire area so they can get to the fire since roads were not passable. My question was, how did they get out?

Another drawback to the forest ranger path was the danger posed by drug dealers during the 1970's who flew planes into the wilderness areas to deliver their drugs under camouflage of the forest. These guys would do anything to protect their enterprise so it became open season on the park rangers and many were shot and killed while investigating suspicious situations. Since my career choice seemed to be gone, I had to do a lot of thinking on my future.

Though I may have wasted time from an academic standpoint at UCONN. My time at UCONN was a great distraction and I was able to succeed socially and helped to give me a sense of worth. It really aided me in staying sane and I look back on that time very fondly.

Return to the Dark Decade

I took a break from discussing the Dark Decade to give both you and myself a break from the morose. My mom and nana were now living together in Stamford, my brother was living in Brookfield with a high school friend and my sister was in New Milford. I would lay my head where I could but would stay with my dad in Ridgefield when home from school. My family was officially dispersed and we would never really be a family unit again.

While I was at school, my dad got married to my stepmother. I had absolutely no intention of going to this wedding and I told them I had some exams and I could not come. It was one of the best decisions I ever made. I just would have felt very uncomfortable and would have felt I betrayed my mother.

My stepmother turned out to be overall fair to me. She seemed to see good in me. She had her own demons to deal with as her own family was very dysfunctional. I did inform her nicely that I will respect her but she is not or never will be my mother and I won't stand for any bashing of my mom.

I noticed that when I brought friends over the house in Ridgefield, it seemed to really upset them. Not sure if they were jealous or if they just did not understand about friends and friendships, because those two never had friends even to their dying days. Once, after my friends left the house one member from my step family started to lecture me about not acting like I'm a part of the new family. I let them know that I never asked for this family and I will be respectful but they should be happy for me that I have friends. I never brought people to that house again and after mom died, I rented the in-law apartment that was attached to the house. I was near them but it felt like I was miles away.

A surprising blessing was my stepmother's sister. She was a widow and her kids had moved out of the house. She had an amazing pool and a big yard, I cut a deal with her to maintain her yard if I could use her pool anytime. I used the pool for several years as a place to relax and have friends over. When I went back to school, I did my homework by the pool. My step aunt loved to travel so she was away a lot and basically, I had my own pool. I really enjoyed this sweet deal.

I kept running during this time. I became close to a group of runners and started participating in road races all around the state and even into parts of New York.   It was an unofficial club we would run, go out to eat together, and talk about breaking our personal best. We ran 5ks, 10ks, ten miles, half marathons and one 20 miler but never a full marathon. I loved running in the various towns along the East Coast, running helped me with my overall health because it is so good for the body and mind.

While living in my apartment in Ridgefield my brother stayed with me when he was out of college on his breaks. We got along well, went to Yankee baseball and Giants football games. Sometimes we went back to Brookfield to hang out with old friends. The Yanik boys were back in town watch out. We both loved Baskin Robbins ice cream and they would have a sale on pints and we would each get a pint after we worked out and then watched a movie. We also played on the same softball team; it was just fun having him around and reminded me how close we were when we were younger.

Mom's DEATH

How could things get any worse? So, to recap, my dad had an affair and left our family, my high school grades went in the toilet, my home was sold, my mom succumbed to mental illness and was committed to a psychiatric hospital, my dad remarried and now was in utopia with his new family. I was twenty years old. My brother was seventeen and my sister was twenty-four. We were so young and so hurt.

Mom was living in Stamford with my nana. On Thanksgiving Day 1977, I drove to Stamford and picked-up mom. We headed to my sister's apartment for dinner in Danbury. My brother joined us and it would be the last time we all saw our mother alive. I would see her a little longer because I drove her back to Stamford. During dinner and on the road home I had a very uneasy feeling within me. I had no idea what that was.

Around 3:30 a.m. I received a phone call from Aunt Mary, telling me that Mom attempted to take her life. I can remember Aunt Mary hysterically trying to explain to me what had happened. It wasn't clear what really happened but I needed to get to Stamford Hospital as quickly as possible. I called my brother, went to pick him up and we both drove to Stamford which was an hour away.

When we arrived at the hospital, we were told mom was not going to make it and they would not let us see her. We still did not know what had happened. All we knew was that she was dying. So, we stayed in the hospital for a bit then went to Aunt Mary's house and waited in a state of shock. Two hour later we got the call that mom was dead. I was basically numb, showing no emotion at all. Saying it was surreal was an understatement. No one uttered a word; we were motionless for what it seemed like hours, but I am sure it was just minutes.

My nana was shell-shocked because she saw something unbearable. Even today I cannot imagine the horror of what she saw as she opened the door and saw my mom's charred burnt body. You see, my mom, in her broken and hopeless state, walked across the street from the apartment to a park with a gallon of gas. She poured it over her body and lit a match. That is shocking enough but my mom, after that attempt, walked a half mile back across the street to my nana's apartment knocked on the door and told my nana she made a mistake, then collapsed. I cannot imagine the pain and horror my lovely nana felt seeing her daughter burnt and half dead on her doorstep. She called for an ambulance and we think she went into shock. My nana did not talk for several days. That afternoon my mom died at the age of 47. She deserved so much better than this.

Mom was the only child, so I had no aunts and uncles on my mom's side. The siblings now had only two adults who cared about us, our nana and a Great Aunt. That number was soon to go down to one. My mom would never see graduations, weddings, spend time with our spouses, or spoil her grandchildren. She was gone, my only consolation was that her pain and hurt was over on this earth.

I never cried. It felt like I was outside of myself. I can't explain it. It was as if I could see myself but not feel anything. Was this a dream, can this really be me living through this horror? I was emotionless and just going through the motions. The funeral was a blur to me with just no recollection. My dad attended but instead of comforting his grieving kids he thought everyone was saying bad things about him. He only proved what a narcissist he was. His kids had lost their mother due to things he did, yet his only concern was that people might be talking about him. Additionally, our relatives on my dad's side never reached out to us. I still can't imagine how they could have been so heartless.

I did not tell anybody back in our hometown about Mom's suicide, but being a small town, I can imagine word got around. Just recently I have been in touch with an old friend from Brookfield, I asked him if he knew how my mom died. He said he did, and he was living in California at that time. If he found out thousands of miles away our neighbors in town knew.

It makes me wonder why the friends I grew up with, and those who knew my mom and were blessed by her kindness when she was in her right mind never reached out to us. My brother was still in town and I was easy to find. I know I acted weird at times as a kid trying to hide my pain. But this was a time to show compassion. Maybe they thought pretending not to know was the best thing.

Maybe I was being too hard or had high expectations, we were all so young and mental illness was not openly discussed. Suicide was hidden even deeper. What would I have done if the roles were reversed, I honestly do not know? I did not want pity or to be treated like a victim. I just wanted compassion and needed a friend. I was so damaged and was in a fog for several months and would not celebrate Christmas. I had the mindset that nothing good will ever happen to me and I rejected some acts of kindness.

I was doubleminded in the way that I wanted people to comfort me, but I hid because of my embarrassment. Man, I was hurting so bad and I was so young. I was losing so much of the things my friends took for granted. Nothing at all made sense, nothing was going well. Who can I turn to for relief? Who can take away this pain? Why did I have to live with the clouds over my head and this fog in front of me? **IT JUST WASN'T FAIR.**

I was shocked and withdrew but headed back to UCONN.   I am not sure how the school found out about it but they were really great. They called me into the dean's office and let me cancel out of some classes that I just couldn't do anymore and refunded my money. They offered to take me to dinner and offered me any counseling sessions if I saw fit. I really appreciated their concern.

My Greek family at the pizza shop were a great comfort to me. They treated me like a king and asked me if I wanted to stay with them over Christmas break. Such kindness. I'm pretty sure I never told them how she died, but just knowing that my mother passed away was enough for them to draw me in closer. My buddy Keith knew the situation and was in constant communication with me at UCONN and back home. Our dorms were close together and one day he came to see me with a free ticket to see Emerson Lake and Palmer. My mom died less than a week ago, should I be going to see a concert in New Haven? He would not accept no, and so we went and for two hours, I was miles away from my pain.

Another good friend, Dallas, invited me out with him often. I think I told him what happened at a high level and he and I became very close. I could not say no to Dallas he was 6 foot 8 inches tall. We went to basketball games; got pizza and we went to see ELO at Madison Square Garden when they actually had a spaceship inside the arena. Great show except for the cello solo that was enough to pull the paint off the wall. Dallas really stood by me then and he would graduate soon after and went on to great things.

I was still in a fog and it was still hard to focus or develop new relationships. I pushed my girlfriend away which I mentioned earlier. I know I could have trusted her and since she lived in Stamford maybe I should have asked her to come to the funeral with me. She would have come for sure and she would have been a big comfort to me. I did not want pity but I should have been open to compassion and enjoyed a great relationship. It was a mistake to close myself off from people who would have provided comfort.

Back at UCONN, a friend of mine told me that a certain girl liked me and she asked me to the pub for beers but, I turned her down. She was a very nice girl and I would sometimes see her around and talk to her. As soon as I rejected her, I said to myself *"what an idiot I am"* but I was so damaged that I would not have been good company. Another girl found out that I like pistachio ice cream and asked me to go to the ice cream parlor where she would treat me to a cone. Again, I was an idiot and turned her down as well. Both nice and innocent friendships pushed to the side. People were being really nice to me but I was too blind and jaded to see their kindness. They must have thought I was a real jerk but I still told no one. In retrospect people saw me in a better light than I saw myself and that is a real shame.

I was not depressed I was shell shocked. I definitely understood the difference. I do not want to minimize what a soldier goes through after battle, but I was beaten up and had nothing left. As low as I got, I knew I would get out of this funk and hey, what else could go wrong? Unfortunately, more pain was on the horizon.

My Nana

Lavinia Trefry was from Baton Rouge, Louisiana, which accounted for my mom being named Etta Mae. She lost her husband at age 50 and her only child lived to the age of 47. She was a rock who loved her grandchildren unconditionally. She was an entrepreneur who owned several hair salons in Stamford. She was a real character when she came to visit us in Brookfield when we were younger. She loved going to the Hearth, an old school restaurant in Brookfield. Everyone in Brookfield knew The Hearth, Vals, Lavelles, Candlewood Inn, Down the Hatch and Widow Browns. In our small town there were not a lot of dining options at that time.

My nana would almost always bring a girlfriend of hers along when she would visit. She loved her cocktails and smoked like a chimney, something I suspect led to her cancer diagnosis. She had helped our family over the years financially and I was told she helped with buying our house in Brookfield. I was very close to her, we seemed to have quite a bond. When she was sick, my loyalty to her came before anything else. It was not a chore it was my pleasure; I adored this woman.

As the school year was ending prior to summer break, I was informed that Nana had Stage 4 bone cancer and was dying. She would soon enter a hospice in Westport, CT. She would die shortly but my visits with her up to that time gave me a lot of great memories. She loved to hear about girls I was dating and what I was up to.   I would drive down to see her and bring her flowers or candy. My best friend, Keith, would come with me and patiently waited while I spent time with her. They stopped her chemo so it was just a matter of time before the end.

She talked to me about Jesus and told me she made her peace with God. She was not afraid to die in fact she seemed to glow as she laid in that bed. As Christians we are not to fear death but know that we are to pass onto heaven and be with Jesus. It affected me so much that I went out and bought a bible and began to read it. She died at age 69 but lived a full life. I really missed her and Mom for years. In fact, you never ever get over it. The one good thing about my nana's death was I got to say goodbye to her and spend some incredible moments with her. Those were two incredible losses in such a short time, for my siblings and me, at such a young age. We now had only Great Aunt Mary as the chief influential relative on my moms' side of the family.

My family was gone. I had my siblings, but any structure or form of a family was gone. I felt totally abandon to think I lost the two people that loved me unconditionally within a year it was devastating. My mom and nana were my biggest advocates and really the only adult family I ever had. For obvious reasons I never connected with my stepfamily, though I continue to be respectful and got along with them. They were never going to fill the void.   I felt I had nobody.

There is absolutely no feeling worse than being unloved. It is the most unbearable feeling a person can endure. It crumbles your self-esteem, confidence and your ability to function day to day. We all want to be understood and loved. It is so calming to know that someone has your back and you can have a person to talk to. I had none of that. Actually, each day felt like I was in a desert looking for water to survive. In my case it was hope and someone to understand not what I went through but the pain I felt. My spirit was crushed but I was more determined to make something out of this misery.

Another funeral again in Stamford, this time for my nana. I went back to my apartment in Ridgefield and began to plot out what I was going to do with a degree that meant nothing and had limited options. Thankfully my dad did not have access to nana's money. She was very loving in making sure that my brother, sister and I would have some finances. I didn't expect anything less. With that money I was able to buy myself a car and have a little savings in the bank.

My stepbrother was a very troubled young man and was severely depressed. Like our family, he lost a parent to suicide. His own father took his life years earlier. I did not know details and it was not my place to ask. John was named after his dad. The young man was hospitalized for a while, but eventually he would succumb to his demons and took his life. He used the same exact method that my mom used to take his life.

The horrors of the Dark Decade were finally over. Unfortunately, the scars and the losses were still very much there. I went to three funerals in three years, two of which were suicides. I was 22 years old; I just saw way too much of life and actually it seemed like hundreds of years of life. I should maybe have shown more emotion, ask for help but I did not want any pity or for people to treat me like a victim. I just ran miles every day and tired myself out to exhaustion. I should have dealt with my feelings because later in life I had to deal with anxiety, depression and PTSD which caused a complete mental breakdown.

Meanwhile, my friends were out of college looking toward their future and careers and going through the normal progressions of life. I was stagnant trying to pick up the pieces of my life and planning my next steps. The progression of life is graduating college, starting a career, getting married and having children. I was pretty much on my own and I was determined to fix this all on my own. I refused to give up but my progression was to be delayed. This really was another source of pain seeing my friends grow up while I had to regroup. I was very hard on myself during this time.

During this time, I picked up a bad attitude which I still have to watch out for today. I had a way of getting really nasty if you were to come at me. If you tried to hurt me, you were in for a barrage of verbal assault. I figured you couldn't possibly hurt me more than I have already been hurt. So, my insults had no bounds and I was tired of being a patsy. This was born out of anger, frustration and helplessness. I got tired of being put in a box with people acting like they knew me or acting like they knew how I felt.

I hate the line when people would tell me I know how you feel and would tell me about something they experience. With all due respect you do not know how I feel, and I would never assume to know how you feel either. As individuals we all handle things so differently and we need to give each person space when it comes to our reactions to things we must bear.

I also did not suffer fools very well. Meaning I had a hard time dealing with people doing silly and careless things and blaming others for the problem. Going through my gauntlet has made me sympathetic but I still do not have a lot of patience with people who do foolish things. My wife points out that trait in me, she is much more understanding in this area than I. I will say I have become more patient and the lord is still working on me in this area.

All the pain, suffering, confusion, abandonment was something on the surface I was able to push to the side but it was tearing me up inside. I was not depressed but I was starting to show signs of agitation and OCD which I really did not deal with and just kept moving through each day.

I believed my behavior would sort itself if I remained busy and focused but all it did was delay the inevitable. Please take your mental health very seriously and do not be ashamed.

Breakdown

Like I said there were only two times when I broke down and wept uncontrollably. When you look at both events, they were out of exhaustion and frustration. The first time this occurred, I was at the Milan's' house. Keith is my closest friend even to this day. His mother, Joan, saw through my poker face and knew I was really hurting. The Milan house was like my sanctuary and not one time did they ever make me feel like I did not belong. I called Mrs. Milan, Joan O. That was my playful way of saying she was as posh as Jackie Kennedy Onassis whom the press dubbed Jackie O in the 1970's.

She played tennis and hobnobbed with the well–to-do of Brookfield. Several times I thought of asking her if I could live with them but then, I thought I would have to breakdown and tell her everything exposing my hurt. She already knew I was hurting it would not be a surprise to her. I just didn't realize it then.

She worked at the tennis club in town. It was called The Bubble, because during the winter they erected an inflatable dome which allowed players to continue enjoying this summer sport. She allowed Keith and me to play tennis at the club. We stuck out like sore thumbs. While everyone came in their tennis whites, Keith and I would show up with some rock band tee shirt and basketball sneakers. When we got bored playing actual tennis, we would play a different game, we called, let's see who can hit the other with the tennis ball. As we made a spectacle of ourselves on the court, I could see Mrs. Milan with her head in her hands. We drove her nuts. I smile now when I think of those days and her patience with us.

The first time I broke down and cried was out of the blue. We were clearing the Milan's' driveway after a big snowstorm. My car was snowed in and we had to get the road shoveled so Mr. Milan could get his car out to get to work the next day. When we finished, I got in my car to back it out of driveway, just like I had done dozens of times before. This time I could not do it. I kept hitting a snowbank, I tried several times with the same result. Finally, I tried one more time and again I hit the snowbank, jammed the car into park started to bang the wheel with my fists and then I cried uncontrollably. It was not the snowbank; I just had enough disappointment and I had to release it. I was tired and unfortunately it just became way too much for me to control.

Keith came to the car and at first looked at me oddly, but he figured it out. He tapped me on the shoulder, told me to move over and he backed the car out. He let me just cry and cry and he never said a word or judged me. He sat in the car with me until I was done sobbing, when I was done, I went in the house and cleaned up my face and then came back out and punched him in the arm. My way of saying thanks. I think he understood my pain. Keith was and is still today such a great friend. I owe a lot to the Milan family for their kindness.

The second breakdown was harder because it came when something really nice was happening to me. I mentioned earlier there was a girl that I really liked spending time with in high school. I did not get to know her until my Senior Year in High school which was weird because I knew some of her friends and talked to them all the time. Since she drove fancy cars, I thought she was a snob, so it was not much of a loss not knowing her. I was totally wrong. We had the same type of sense of humor, we both loved the same music going to concerts and reading. This girl always had a book in her hand, I think she was born with a book in her hand. Plus, she was really easy to talk to.

The first time I talked to her was on a field trip that very few people went on. As we walked around the museum she chose to walk and talk with me. She then dashed away but continued this cat and mouse game until we got on the bus. So, I sat down on the bus and she sat in the seat right behind me. The bus was empty, she could have sat anywhere but she plopped herself next to me. She asked me if I was hungry and we went into the deli bought a bag of pistachio nuts. The idea was to share but she basically ate most of the bag. My revenge was to throw my shells at her. We had a pistachio shell fight. That began our friendship, we then hung out a lot in school.

We hung out so much that people thought she was my girlfriend and I repeatedly told them we were just friends. I really enjoyed spending time with her but my self-esteem was in the toilet.   I never thought I was good enough for her. For whatever reason my so-called friends discouraged me from seeing her as well. Looking back, they had ulterior motives. If people asked me, I would tell them I like her and made no bones about it. The only person I did not tell was her, but she knew and still wanted to hang out with me. It was not a mystery that I liked her. I was also very naïve. I always held the belief that I was not good enough for her.

Before I headed back to UCONN I had a severe break in my nose and had to have major reconstructive surgery. I had a deviated septum plus damaged cartilage in my nose. I could not breath through my nose, so it was pretty serious. As I walked in to the hospital's check-in area, she walked right by me in a lab coat. I did not call out to her and she did not see me. I was pretty resigned to the fact it was not in the cards for us so I actually chuckled. The whole two ships passing in the night thing. She was doing her Senior College Internship as a medical tech student and she really looked as cute as ever.

As funny as it sounds the hospital was a relief from my home life. My mom was in the psychiatric hospital and that was painful enough. My dad really wanted to start his new life with his new family and wanted me out. So, believe it or not this was a respite despite surgery. I got to rest plus they had Lorna Dunes for snack, I had to put on the Yanik charm to get them instead of Fig Newtons.

As I laid in bed, she comes around the corner into my room with the biggest smile ever. I guess she saw my name on some roster and decided to see me. She looked radiant and seeing her winning smile just made the pain I was about to encounter bearable. We were both so happy to see each other it had been a while. It was great we joked around like old times and it was just us no other influences to get in the way of us spending time together in a hospital. I was in the hospital for three days and she came down often to see me each day. We played cards and just talked and I know we both missed each other.

My roommate was an Australian guy who I befriended and he told me I had a beautiful girlfriend. I began to tell him she was not my girlfriend and he stopped and said, *"Mate do you see how she looks at you?"* I wanted to sneak out of my room and visit her in the room they gave her in the hospital to stay. I really thought about it but I really did not want to get her in trouble. Overall, I was on cloud nine and I knew she really did care for me very much. She gave me her phone number and really wanted to get together. During those days in the hospital my life seemed so right I was oblivious to the troubles outside. It really meant a lot to me that she spent that time with me. All my troubles seemed not to matter.

I left the hospital a day earlier and when I talked to her on the phone, she said she missed seeing me in the hospital. If I knew she would keep visiting I would have broken my nose again just so we could hang out. I am not kidding. Since I had to recover, we had to delay getting together but we talked on the phone every night until we got together. Those were as joyful as her visits in the hospital, we just clicked together. I was so happy. I know she was seeing someone and so was I but it did not matter. We talked a lot on the phone and caught up, I always thought when it was just us, we got along great.

I just wanted to spend time with her and have fun. If there was a romance that would be good if not that was good too. I liked and respected her and I just wanted her to be happy. Above all she was my friend. I guess love is wanting the best for someone. What I liked about her so much was she really reminded me of my nana the same sense of humor, both easy to talk to, and they both loved to read. I wish that they could have met that would have been a hoot. The day we had a date my dad and I got in a major fight. In his haste to get me out of the house things got really heated.

I should have delayed the date or have been honest with her, but why should I lose out on this amazing opportunity with someone I cared about. On the way to pick her up I wanted to tell her what was going on and I knew someday I would get through this and right now I really need a good friend in my life. But I never said those words. I did not want to drag her into my darkness, and I would not tolerate her feeling sorry for me. I could have used the pity angle but that was not my style and she deserved better.

During our time together that night I was not the same person I was in the hospital or on the phone with her. I was very sad and my mind was preoccupied with my horrible life. I could have not been much fun. I drove her to her house at the end of the night and kissed her which turned out to be a kiss goodbye. I sabotaged the date and told her I cannot handle this right now and gave her no background why I acted that way. She stepped out of the car and I never saw or spoke to her again.

On my way home I cried and cried even when I got in the driveway in Ridgefield I cried for a long time. I sat there thinking that I was never going to have something good happen to me. I had just had enough of losing out on things, I was crushed. Though this was not my greatest disappointment during that time it just tipped the scale. Something so cool as us rekindling whatever it was meant to be had to take a backseat to my crappy life. She was the last person who I ever wanted to hurt or have think bad of me.

I never got to tell her how much her visits to me in the hospital meant and that her desire to reconnect was awesome and heartwarming. It was a light in a very dark time for me seeing her smile and laughing was better medicine then the doctors could ever give me. I was in a place where my emotions were just spent, I had nothing to give. So, I ripped the bandage off, she was on her way to doing great things in her career and I was not sure where I was going to sleep the next day. I did the right thing, three months later my mom died.

Years later, when I got on the right track, I thought to contact her and apologize and explain my irrational behavior. I didn't do it; time had moved on and I needed to get out of the past and I forgot her. It really hurt to lose my friend we were real good friends. It was a real shame. I still at times look back and miss her friendship. Like from the start all I wanted for her was to be happy.

At times I felt alone, but God would send people in my life just at the right time with the right assistance. He knew how bad this all hurt and understood my pain. I also started reading the bible at this time and also any book I could get on the greatest leader of the 20th century, Winston Churchill. Talk about guts, Churchill and the British nation defined guts. I was going to be a mini-Churchill and climb out of the pit I was in.

Trials and Temptations

> *2 Consider it pure joy, my brothers and sisters,[a] whenever you face trials of many kinds, 3 because you know that the testing of your faith produces perseverance. 4 Let perseverance finish its work so that you may be mature and complete, not lacking anything. 5 If any of you lacks wisdom, you should ask God, who gives generously to all without finding fault, and it will be given to you. James 1:2-5*

Reading about Churchill put a charge in me, I was not yet a believer but under no circumstances was I going to let my family issues define me. I stopped abusing drugs and alcohol, I still would drink but I never drank and did drugs alone anymore. I was running and playing basketball and softball in various sports.

The Dark Decade was complete, and I was given the gift of Grace from God. Things just fell into place for me and I had a sense of confidence and a mission. I was down but not out, there were other plans in my life. God had plans for me and I had to give him control.

Prayer of Thankfulness

> *God thanks for walking with us when the chips are down, when our pain is indescribable, when we cry and it seems nobody is listening, not even you. Only you and your word can be the true comforter in our woes. You were always there to wipe away a tear and pick me up.*

Signs of my Illness

Unfortunately, one of the things I was never able to do was grieve. The events came so fast and furious, I just never took the time to reflect and talk to someone about the traumas that affected me. The dark decade would catch up with me later in life because I did not learn how to grieve. I did not have an adult to guide me, so I did the next best thing and that was to focus on my comeback and stay very busy. Nothing wrong with that there just really needed to be a balance of recovery and comeback.

Staying busy and exercising delayed the inevitable in my case of falling into depression and dealing with anxiety. From a medical perspective I had thyroid and hormone issues and a low metabolic rate which had an adverse effect on my health and my mental well-being. In the eighties it manifested itself with OCD where I would double and triple check things and ruminate over situations in my head. It was hard to remove thoughts from my mind and I repeated questions often.

Later in life, it would then progress to me being agitated and losing patience quickly. Traffic was especially hard for me to cope with and I felt hemmed in the car and this could lead to panic attacks. If you have ever had a panic attack, you can understand that your initial reaction is to think you're having a heart attack. You sweat, your heart is beating a million miles a minute and you feel extreme panic. You just want it to go away. I went to the ER several times thinking I had a heart attack and realizing it was a panic attack.

As the years went on the stress at work was unbearable and things, I loved to do like coaching sports became an annoyance without joy. My sense of humor began to include sarcasm which were hurtful to people I loved. I was not always a treasure to be around.

I also started to feel ashamed and annoyed with myself for not handling my emotions better. If I could get through the Dark Decade this had to be a piece of cake. I was very hard on myself plus I had a wife and two young children I did not want to disappoint. These events would come and go and I did not deal with them instead I thought that on my own I could overcome them and at times I was able to pull myself out of it but I really needed to get help. The pressure I put on myself to get better made things much worse. I never gave myself room to see that I was ill.

This was progressive over decades and while I thought I was fine, layers of myself were peeling away with each struggle. It finally came to a head around 2016 where I basically lost my way for two years. As you will read in the next parts of the book, I did get my life back on track after college and became a Christian but I did not take good care of my mental health over the years and it cost me. If you or a friend needs help, get it and do not be ashamed.   Don't let it spiral out of control like I did, you can and will get better.

Comeback

One of the great confidence boosters for me was the discovery that girls liked me. I discovered it really after high school, maybe they liked me in high school as well, I was oblivious to it. By the time I got to UCONN my eyes were wide open. I had several relationships during that time. It was unnerving and surprising at first but helped me so much to see that I had worth. Besides relationships I just got along with women in general. I was not a ladies' man I was always a gentleman and honored my mom and nana in that manner. I definitely was no saint, but I could not degrade anyone by just seeing a person as a sex object. I was taught, from an early age, to respect women.

A lot of my relationships were just friends at first and we would gain trust and become an item. I never understood the boyfriend-girlfriend thing at an early age. I found it restrictive and way too much drama. At UCONN a girl who was in some of my classes, and who would later come back into my life was an interest that never manifested itself at school. She would sit next to me in class, but she always was with some guy, so I thought they were together. When it was cold her nose and cheek became an adorable pink. I would see her again after college.

I have for the most part really fond memories of the girls that I spent time with. I think it might have been because I saw my mother or nana in most of them. These girls were kind, sweet, intelligent and really easy to talk with. I really enjoyed drama free relationships and most of my dates were simple walks, going to a park, a jog or just basically hanging out. I do not recall ever getting stoned or drunk with any girlfriend I spent time with.

I loved talking and being with woman they were easier to talk with and much more interesting than guys. I found the whole macho guy thing really dull; I was not interested in talking about how many girls I slept with or my high school glory days. Since I was raised mostly by women, I just naturally could talk to them with no fear and the stigma of feeling unworthy was gone. It is disappointing to think that I never had a strong male role model in my life. Not my father, no teacher, no coach, nor uncle ever took time to mentor me. I imagine that many men can identify with my experience. That would change when I met Jesus.

After graduating from UCONN, I moved back into the apartment which was attached to my dad's house, but I was light years away. I would not even use their washing machines, I wanted and had complete autonomy. Ridgefield was a more affluent town than Brookfield, but it was a nice break from Brookfield which I would go back to from time to time.

In Ridgefield they had nice parks and the town bordered the town of Pound Ridge, NY. During that time, I played a lot of golf, played in several basketball leagues and softball leagues so I was very active with that and going to road races on the weekend. A lot of celebrities lived there, and I ran into the actor Robert Vaughan, Daryl Hall of the group Hall and Oates and actor Alan Arkin. It was your typical affluent Fairfield County town with a nice downtown area.

I started a job in Norwalk, CT as a production control planner working again for Perkin Elmer. I needed money and this was at least a start. The company had sophisticated machines which made the computer wafers that made computer chips. They had a clean room since the machines were very sensitive to any dirt. My group planned out spare parts for customers who already had machines. We also had rush orders that had to go out daily for any machine that went down, we ran around like crazy getting the parts, sending them through quality control and shipping them. I was a gopher for the most part, but it paid the bills. I guess it could have been worse.

Thinking back to third grade when the teacher asked me what I wanted to be when I grew up, I'm pretty sure I did not say Production Control Planner. There was nothing wrong with the job it was just not what I wanted to do for the rest of my life. I had to come up with another plan and I had to think quickly. I did not hate the job I just did not see myself doing this for more than a few years at the most. My friend Keith was in the same position in New Hampshire, his family moved there so they could be closer to his dads' job.

Keith would come back to visit, or I would go up to Portsmouth, NH quite often. They bought an old New England style home and it was walking distance to the downtown area, a recreation area and the water. Back then you could get a lobster roll for five bucks, I really liked going there. Plus, I got to hang with Joan O. Keith's brother Craig and I would sneak into the pool at the University of New Hampshire.

Keith was working in a light bulb factory and made the decision to join the Air Force. I actually took the physical and passed but never enlisted. It was one of many decision points that could have changed the direction of my life. Because of my eyesight I could not qualify as a pilot so I decided against it. Keith benefited from his time in the Air Force and has had a successful career as a commercial airline pilot.

My work environment was an extension of high school with a mix of Peyton Place. The guys I worked with were really immature and tried to get out of work like kids skipping classes. They would fudge timesheets for each other go out get drunk and race their souped-up hot rods. These were not just young guys doing these things some were grown men acting like children. One guy never came back after lunch, he would leave for hours and come back sign out or have someone else fudge his record.

Everyone was sleeping with everyone else. Three of my bosses were having open affairs with girls much younger than themselves. It was so obvious they did not try to hide it. I never watched soap operas, but each day some drama was happening. If this is corporate life, then I was greatly dismayed. There were two guys who were above the fray one was my co-worker and the other was my friend Willie with whom I played basketball often.

My co-worker was getting married soon so he was very responsible, and we hung out a bit. He had a boat and we would go fishing or water skiing on Lake Candlewood. He would joke around but he took his job seriously and we would both shake our heads at some of the things people did at work. Since we had to work with every department, we knew everybody in the production department. We worked together very well as a team.

Willie was the best basketball player I ever played against, he played Division One basketball but got injured and lost his scholarship. At this time, I was reading the bible really for common sense reasons. It was a best-selling book, I loved to read so I became very curious what was inside this book that had been around forever.

Willie was a Christian and was to become an ordained Baptist preacher. Willie is African American. He would speak to me about Jesus and I listened, and he would answer my questions, I really respected what he had to say. He planted the seed in my heart and as we talked, I still had not totally bought-in, but I was open. We went to lunch together and he ordered a beer during one meal. I did not want a beer but afterwards he felt so guilty that he drank a beer in front of me. He was worried that I would have thought less of him as a Christian. I thought that was kind of touching. He told me that one day I would accept Christ, and he was right.

So where do I go with my future. I notice that Western Connecticut State University (WESTCONN), the school I should have originally gone to, opened up a new computer science department and business school. I went to visit the business school and ran into the Dean in the hall. He actually took the time to talk to me. What a great guy! He proudly walked me around the new building and we laid out a plan for me to get a degree in Management Information Systems. The only problem was with me working and it was going to take forever going to night school. His projection was 1986, I had to cut that in half, that would be too long for me. I had to devise a plan to get a degree in Management Information System at the least cost possible in both time and money.

It seemed like I would end up attending every state school in Connecticut. I started with some night classes. This was to get my feet wet and I loved it. A lot of people were working and going to school at night, so it was also great socially and I started to cultivate great relationships. I still had to come up with a plan to get out earlier. The College Level Examination Program (CLEP), is a group of standardized tests created and administered by the College Board. These tests assess college-level knowledge in various subject areas and by passing the exams one could earn credits without taking the course. I was very fortunate enough to pass several CLEP exams and earn the credits. This saved a lot of time and money and put me farther ahead than I would have been.

This time I had a purpose with my education and I was able to put elements of the Dark Decade in the rear-view mirror for now. On the job, we had just hired a new guy named Alan. He was from Brooklyn and I was not really sure why he took this job. He was super to me and for some reason he took an interest in to me and we hung out a bit and went to some Yankee games. He kept telling me I needed to leave this job and could do so much better. We worked in a factory basically, but he was always dressed in three-piece suits and was constantly smoking.

The funny part was he had some very shady connections. Every day his friend Sonny would call and never say Hello. He would just ask if Alan was there, pretty rudely. Alan would go into the office lock the door and talk to Sonny. One day Alan came to me with a proposition, would I like to make a thousand dollars a week, he asked. I listened as he told me about how each weekend, he and others rented out space and sold high end women's clothing. I asked him two questions, where did the clothes come from? Was this linked to the mob? On both questions he pleaded the fifth, so I declined the offer. Alan continued to support me in my quest to do better for myself which led to my next step. I sidestepped my potential time with organized crime.

I figured I could get out in 1984 if I were able to take classes Tuesday and Thursday afternoon. I held a carrot for my coworker, I told him that I would cover Monday mornings and Friday afternoons if I could leave Tuesdays and Thursdays at noon so I could take classes. If we did that, he could leave for ski trips or boating early Friday. He loved the idea and our boss approved the idea. My co-worker loved his weekends and it was a perfect solution.

For almost two years I went to school Monday and Wednesday night and also during the afternoons on Tuesday and Thursday. I was extremely busy never home, but I had my life back. I felt like that little boy in Darien cutting deals and in control of my destiny. I was still playing in basketball leagues, softball leagues, golf and running in road races on the weekend. Plus, I still had exclusive access to my step aunt's pool in Ridgefield. I would still read a lot between all of this and the Gospels began to make more and more sense to me. Jesus was becoming more real.

Going back to school at night and during the day, you get a variety of people. The regular students, working people, MBA students, married woman and older woman whose kids have grown up. One girl from high school was getting her MBA at nights and we did a couple of things together. She talked me into going to our high school reunion after telling me a certain person was going to be there. She did not show up and I wanted to leave but I did hang out. I have not been to a reunion since.

I was getting all A's and really enjoyed school. I was in a sense reborn I proved to myself that I was a good student. I was really good in finance and maybe I should have chosen that route. I think I was good in finance because I always found a way to stretch a buck and knew how to make money. I was also cheap. One of the finance teachers took an interest in me and we would get a soda or coffee together. This woman drank Pepsi literally like water and she honored me with a merit certificate and put me in the Finance Honor Society. That may not sound like a big deal, but to me it was validation. I was getting my life back. I was proving to myself that I could accomplish goals and balance a hectic schedule.

I was in multiple study groups mostly with the night students or the older ladies whose kids were grown up. I guess I still looked young because one day one of the undergrads sheepishly asked me to be in her study group. She was probably about 19 or 20 and was with some of the other honor students. I was either 24 or 25. Maybe she drew the short straw and was the one pegged to ask me. I almost cried when she asked me. After the lowness I felt in high school over my poor grades and the disappointment of losing out my preferred colleges I was going to hang with the smart kids. They were also all girls in the study group which made it that much better. I told them I would be honored to join, and she gave me a big smile.

We would meet in a designated area in a study lounge and work on some problems and projects together. It was during the early part of the 1980's and they all loved Cyndi Lauper, Pat Benatar and Duran Duran. Not exactly my cup of tea, I liked the Who, Yes and King Crimson. When the study room was empty and it was just us, they would play their music. To me it was like fingernails on the chalkboard, but they were so nice and kind, so I let it slide. They also always brought the best snacks, sometimes homemade.

Though my mom and nana were not alive they were still a major influence on my behavior especially with women. I will admit that, for a period of time, I took advantage of certain situations I was in, mostly after drinking. After really hurting someone, I was not serious about, I changed my behavior. I knew my mom and nana would be very angry with me if they saw me treat a person badly. I eventually realized that I really cannot drink or do drugs at the rate I was. If I continued, I would go broke and at some point, grow dependent on either drugs or alcohol or both. I saw what drugs was doing to some of my friends and wanted no part of this life. I would eventually quit.

When I was around twelve my mother and I were heading into a department store called Caldor. I rushed ahead and ran into a store cutting a woman off at the door. My mom was furious she scolded me for being rude and made me apology to the lady and henceforth I would open doors for women as they come into a building. A practice I taught my son and still follow today. Etta Mae did not play when it came to manners and I might still have the bruises to show for it.

My mom and nana's expectations of me really came to light in a situation that occurred during these college years. I was in a class with the night students and I was working on a marketing campaign with a group. One of the members of the group was a married woman with a couple of kids. She was a couple years older than me and we got along really well. As the school year moved on, we seemed to work together on all the projects, and she started to tell me that her marriage was falling apart and that she married way too young. I was very naïve. We exchange numbers and she would call me at night while her husband was out.

After class a bunch of us were going to get a drink at a local pub. So, I was to drive, and everyone got in my car and she was in the back seat. At the last minute two of the people decided to take their own cars leaving us alone. She moved into the front seat and began to tell me that she cared for me and wanted to spend time with me. Trust me it was a very tempting offer, she really looked good that night. I wonder if I was set up but again, I was naïve.

Believe me, I was really tempted but after what happened in my family, I could not get into an affair with a married woman, no matter the status of her marriage. I told her I was flattered but I did not feel comfortable. I drove her to her car and I said goodnight. It was very hard to pass this up, but it was the right thing to do. Soon after, I saw her in the supermarket with her two kids. I knew right then that I made the right decision turning her down. I hope she saved her marriage. If I had taken her up on the offer, I would have been the biggest hypocrite in the world. And I hate hypocrisy.

Unfortunately, I continued sabotaging some really great relationships. I reconnected with my pistachio ice cream friend from UCONN, we dated a few times and I really enjoyed it. Just a really great girl but with my baggage and my inability to accept something good for myself, I turned her away. Some of these girls I dated would ask me why things ended so quickly and I really did not have a good answer for them. Anyone getting too close would eventually learn about my past and I think it would have freaked people out. Telling someone about myself was really putting myself out there making myself vulnerable. I think most of all I wanted to avoid any discussion or thoughts about the past I wanted to escape.

As life was progressing my friends started to get married and I went to about a dozen weddings. Of course, if I brought someone or went stag, I got the question when was I going to get married. I had absolutely no desire to get married. I never had a good example of marriage and actually some of the couples pushing me to get married are not together anymore. I liked my freedom and liked dating around but it did hurt that I could not give myself to one specific person. Since I did not get married until I was thirty-five, I continued along this pattern for quite some time.

I was extremely busy and there were only classes offered on the Monday, Wednesday and Friday schedule that I needed in order to graduate. I would reduce my graduation timeline down even more and I could graduate two years ahead of plan. So, I requested a leave of absence from work that would run the school year calendar. Perkin Elmer would still pay my tuition and health care during that time so I got my friend who was the big boss' secretary to put the request in for me. She put in a good word for me so I had that in my pocket. I had it written in a way that I could come back anytime. It was a sweet deal. I should have been a lawyer after all.

My dad retired at 55 years old and was moving to Hendersonville, NC. Hendersonville was a hot retirement community in the mountains of North Carolina. It is right near Asheville which is very eclectic and artist come from around the world to settle there. I really admire artsy people and their ability to create. The North Carolina mountains are quite spectacular during the fall season. The colors are as spectacular as any New England fall.

With dad moving I would have to find a place to live and work at the same time to pay for expenses. I discussed my situation with a classmate, Joe, and he suggested I apply for Resident Assistant (RA) job. He was already an RA so he told me he would put in a good word for me. I thought about whether I would really want to live in a dorm with college kids but I was cheap so the idea of free room and board put me over the top. Once I realized I would also get my own room I interviewed and got the job. My reasoning was if I had to find a place to live, I may have to rent a room anyway and I would avoid that cost.

Joe started school later in life and was around my age. I think he was in the military for a period of time. He and I would go to New York City together several times and he knew it like the back of his hand. Joe was a great golfer and we played together often. Biggest Springsteen fan in the world, he had every record, every bootleg known to mankind. He was a good guy.

Working at Perkin Elmer was really getting old to me and I just wanted out. I am thankful for what Perkin Elmer did for me, but I needed to move on plus the commute on Route 7 from Norwalk to Danbury was really becoming a bear. So, I started my last year of college in the fall of 1983 living in a dorm as an RA.

Life was good at this point the last remnant of the Dark Decade was moving to North Carolina. I was thrilled to see him go. God put so many people in my path to allow me to get my life back on track it was just laid out too well for it to be luck. The job, going back to school, CLEPPING classes and getting my computer science degree two years ahead of schedule were just blessings.

I entered my RA job at WESTCONN with all A's. Unfortunately, I did take a really hard class in statistical analysis which I got a C. I found the class interesting but was very challenging, I still graduated with high honors despite that blemish. I am not bragging I was so thankful and blessed to make this comeback.

I felt a bit odd, at times, living in a dorm at my age now but it was a blessing. My brother lived in the dorm before I got there so they knew I was older. A lot of coeds, for an older guy this was just too tempting and though I was not perfect I really did not want to lead anyone on or take advantage of the situation. I wanted to do school the right way this time. I coached the girls flag football team and I organized the inter-dorms snowball fight, but I really just felt out of place and I just did not want to take advantage of the situation at hand.

I did become interested in one girl that lived in my friend Joe's dorm. For whatever reason when I saw her my heart melted. She was a petite, blonde girl only about 5' 2" and I just did not understand why she turned my heart to jelly. We were friendly but she was so young, seven years younger than me. Later in life it would not be a big deal but in college no way. I was told she felt the same way but it just was not right. I would run into her again later and she would still melt my heart.

On a lighter note, a friend of mine asked me to keep an eye on the game room in the student union with him one night. He was short staffed due to the Ramones concert that night, so I helped out. It was very slow that night due to the concert, so I started playing pinball as I played game after game as I looked to my left there was Joey Ramone watching me play. Joey wanted to blow off some steam before he went on stage, so he and I played pinball. A weird guy but he was very nice, as they left for the show, I told him and Marky Ramone to have a great show. For a bit of time, I was a Ramone groupie. So cool.

As I worked my way through my last year, my advisor called me to tell me that they were going to waive a class so if I wanted, I could graduate in December 1983. At first, I was really excited at the opportunity but since I had planned on being in school for the whole year I did not really apply for any jobs. So, if I left, I would go back to Perkin Elmer to the type of job I had before. Here would have been a good time to have had a male role model to discuss these options with.

I really wrestled with this decision for a whole week. I also was very serious about applying to law school. I had the grades and the test scores, and it was something I always wanted to do. I believe God would have honored either decision in my life. Obviously, money was the big consideration. I could have stayed another semester and applied for jobs in both finance and management information systems. If I had stayed, I would have also applied to law schools and for other jobs. So, another decision tree that would have an effect on my life.

My other thought was my high school and college friends were moving on with their lives they were getting married and having children. With my situation I did not feel bad about going back to school, but there is a part of me that still hurt from losing those valuable years which delayed my life. I figured it was time to move on from college and go back to work. I would almost be thirty when I would have graduated so I decided not to pursue law school.

Before I started my job at Perkin Elmer, I was offered two jobs. One was with the CIA, yes that CIA. I passed all the security screens and thought about it very seriously but I decided it was not for me. My wife laughed when I told her this story, she thinks that I cannot keep a secret. I would have probably been killed or in jail in some foreign country for divulging the master plan. I also had an offer from Ross Perot's company EDS, it was a great offer, but they wanted me to move to Detroit and that was definitely not for me. I worked with several consulting companies and eventually joined IBM for most of my career.

Salvation

John 3:16-1716 For God so loved the world, that he gave his only begotten Son, that whosoever believeth in him should not perish, but have everlasting life.17 For God sent not his Son into the world to condemn the world; but that the world through him might be saved.

The more I read the bible the more the word of God opened my eyes to who Jesus is and how much I was truly loved by God. Though I was on the right track with my life something was still missing. I wanted to give my heart to God and accept Christ as my savior. I thought there was some magic way of doing it, so on December 2nd 1984, I approached some Christians who were selling Christmas trees down the road from where I lived. I knew the guys, so I went to them and directly asked them, *"How do I accept Christ?"* That evening I accepted Jesus Christ. It was the best decision that I ever made. We have free will and I came to Christ under my own free will. Nobody even had to witness to me or try to hammer ideas in my head. I did not join a cult or some mystical troupe I just wanted to follow Christ. I felt a sense of peace that passes all understanding. I knew my creator.

God does not want your belongings, your money, your sacrifice, he just wants you. Regardless of rich or poor, color of your skin, education level or any other characteristic. God just wants you. In the book of Mark, the verse below is powerful in its simplicity and the question it asks.

"What good is it for someone to gain the whole world, yet forfeit their soul?" Mark 8:35

My life was now settled, I just gave my heart to Christ and things just made sense. I was getting multiple job offers while I was still working at Perkin Elmer and I was very busy with my running group and friends. When I went back to Perkin Elmer, they moved me to the Ridgefield Office which made for a shorter commute. I also moved into a house with my brother and a few of his friends which helped to keep my expenses low.

One of my challenges was seeing God as my father. Since I neither had an engaged father nor a positive male role model it took some doing to totally trust God as my father. It was quite a stretch for me to accept that someone cared about me no matter what sins I committed or who I was. I have closed the gap on this challenge, but I still need to close it further. I still struggle with it even today that is the main reason I dedicated myself to being the best dad I could be. While I close the gap, Jesus understands and still loves me and helps me to close this gap which is on my side not his. Today, I have no patience for lousy fathers, it is so irresponsible and disgusting to me.

In my life as in Jesus' life, women played a major role. Jesus was raised by a strong woman, and when he was crucified and right after his resurrection it was two women who were by his side while the men hid in their homes afraid of the Romans. That is why today I am able to recognize and appreciate the women who helped me in my life because I truly do not know where I would be without them. My mom, Nana, Mrs. Milan and many other great ladies opened up their hearts to me when I needed help.

Christian Life

I now knew my creator and I wanted to follow him. I felt God's presence and I continued to think about Jesus and talk to him throughout the day. I lost the desire for drugs and alcohol and I stopped gambling.

I began attending an evangelical church. Going to a charismatic church was so new to me, I had never been to church like this before. The churches I was exposed to growing up were more formal and very low energy, if I can say that. This was a whole new world. I like to simplify the exuberance of the charismatic Christian by comparing it to someone who goes to a concert or a sporting event, but the Christian is rooting for Jesus instead of a performer or a team. It is enthusiastic worship.

I learned a lot from the preaching and teaching. I assimilated into the church pretty quickly. I became an usher, taught Sunday school and worked with the youth group. I made some great friends and we also played in several softball and basketball leagues. Overall, it was a great church to begin my walk and learn about Jesus. I stayed at that church about four years and then was transferred by IBM and moved to Farmington, CT.

One of the kids in the youth group was this boy named Ben. Ben was my mini-me, we had the same exact sense of humor. We would imitate movie scenes from our favorite movies and make up songs with very stupid lyrics. We were both Yankee fans and I was so sad to hear that he had passed away at the age of 42 due to cancer. He honestly was one of my favorite people ever. I loved that kid.

People started to know me in the church, and I began to date a girl whose parents were leaders in the church. Of all the relationships I ever had this is the only one I regret. Since I was dating a well- known girl, some people in the church thought it was their right to know my business. I don't like people who think they know me or have any right to get into my business. I was in my late twenties and I was not married. Oh, the horror! It was the silliest stigma I had to deal with and at times I thought it was humorous but other times it was truly annoying and none of anybody's business.

I thought my girlfriend's family was the perfect family because they played the role perfectly. I was fooled for a period of time. When you looked behind the curtain what you saw was extremely arrogant people and a high level of hypocrisy. I was older and I did not fit their mold for a potential son-in-law, so they put pressure on her to end it. I felt bad for her and I guess with my newness to this world I let my guard down. Usually, I would have just moved on, but for some reason I held on trying to prove some point. I was wrong, I definitely did not love her, and I missed out on other relationships at this time. When it ended it did not end well and I regret that. The silver lining of all of this was I met my lovely wife Michelle in the same church.

I cannot stand hypocrisy or people who think they are better than others. We all do hypocritical things, but we should recognize it and change. We just cannot live like we are above anyone. I have found that having money, position, or just pride can fuel that elite attitude. They practice a "false humility", they act humble while they walk around with an applause sign over their head. The Bible is very specific on this with the statement that the "last will be first".   Remember God wants us, not our stuff. Our stuff isn't coming with us when we die.

The experience with that family did not interfere with my relationship with Jesus. People are people even church people. They have faults just like non-believers. Yes, they and I should act much better, but we are flawed humans who are in need of a savior and we have the ability to forgive one another. People will let you down Christ never will. We must turn and focus on Jesus, he is perfect. You and I will let people down.

God continued to bless me during this time. Through a friend at the church, I was able to rent a house in New Fairfield across the street from a pond where I could swim and fish. My neighbors across the street went to my church and we became friends and they allowed me access to the pond at any time. I loved it, I was able to enjoy summer sports and ice skating in the winter. This family had a little boy who loved to join me when I would go fishing, he'd call me Kurty-Kurt and we became quite good friends.

When they moved out, I rented their house at a very low rate. I used to swim across the pond which was a distance of a mile going to the other side and back. When my friend's mother happened to be at the house while I was doing my swim across the lake and back, she would nervously watch me the entire time. When I completed the swim, there was relief on her face. God continued to bless me as he led me through life, and we should not forget his small blessings. It proves he cares so much for us.

Marriage

What I was not ready for as a new Christian was the hang up and pressure people put on those who were not married. Did they read the Bible and see that many of Christ's most loyal followers were not married? It seemed like in church-culture the girls who went off to Christian college were supposed to find "the one" that God had for them. I cannot imagine being a young girl having all this pressure. I advise my kids, to be settled in a career and know themselves before they jump into marriage.

I am not against young marriages; I was really against the pressure people put on these kids. Heaven forbid you should be in your late twenties and not married like I was. If I heard the term "the one" or soul mate one more time I was going to puke. Based on my past and seeing some of my Christian and non-Christian friends' marriages it just did not seem like something I really wanted. A lot of those marriages fell apart so what was I missing. I went from dating quite a bit to people in church thinking I might not be heterosexual, or I was too lazy or shallow to support a wife.

If I just talked to a girl, I had people ask me what I was thinking. They want to know if I was thinking marriage. I think you should mind your own business. I was constantly being fixed up and it really felt a bit crazy. The only person in the church who didn't pressure me was the mom of two of my good friends. Mrs. Strohm had my best interest at heart. She didn't pressure me about marriage, but our conversations were about the blessings of marriage. When she did speak to me about getting married, she added that I should do it before she retires to the south. I am very happy to report that Mrs. Strohm came to my wedding before retiring. I know she prayed for me a lot, what a great lady.

I never bought into the notion that God has only one direction for our lives, in marriage, career, where you live, or the college you chose. I think that really limits God and puts a lot of pressure on the individual. What if I make the wrong choice will my life go in the dumpster, if we are to think that way, we really limit God's mercy and love for us. Unless it is sin or disobedience, I totally believe God is looking out for us as we go through life's challenges.

Before I got married God put two women in my path that was not by chance but possibly for marriage. At Perkin Elmer I was called into human resources to sign some papers for health care. The girl from UCONN with the rosy cheeks, that I was very interested in, took a temporary job there before going on a mission's trip. She was working with a Christian group and took a job at Perkin Elmer before she went on mission in Europe. Mind you we had never actually spent a lot of time together at UCONN, but I could sense her interest. She definitely knew who I was, and I was very interested in her.

I told her I was a Christian and she was very happy and discussed our faith quite a lot. We hung out a lot at work and talked to her a lot on the phone. In my mind this was not a coincidence, God put this person in my path. I chickened out and backed away from this gift. Even though I could see us together, I did not have enough faith or trust in God to move forward. I know that I hurt her. She was a super girl and I am convinced that God blessed her with someone else.

The second opportunity came when at church and we were having a multiple service conference. During the service I looked over and saw the girl I melted over at WESTCONN, her being out of school made the age difference much more doable. When I saw her, I felt exactly the same way as I did those years back. My heart turned to jelly; I was so starry eyed. Unfortunately, I was in a regrettable relationship at the time and my girlfriend was with me while I chatted with my WESTCONN friend making it uneasy for us to talk and reconnect.

She was a Christian, working as a flight attendant and showed me pictures of her travels. I could see the disappointment in her face when she saw I was with someone else and after the meetings I never saw her again. I was even more disappointed and really regret not moving forward with her and pursuing that opportunity. I paid the price by staying in a failing relationship and I really thought God was done providing me potential mates. Both opportunities were definitely not coincidences and at that point I really started to think about marriage and the next phases in my life. We serve a merciful God and he would give me another shot. The third time would be a charm with Michelle.

Unfortunately, I returned to my bad habit of dating girls and cutting when I thought it was getting too close. I know I hurt several girls and I was not proud of my behavior. One girl actually asked me to marry her. I had to decline the offer. Then came Michelle, we started dating and I felt really good about us. Instead of me cutting it off she did, she got scared but I knew it was not over. I really had a good feeling about her, and I was patient with her.

I was transferred to the Hartford Branch while working for IBM. I moved to Farmington, CT and dated a couple of girls that were basically weird. I finally had enough, and I wanted to get married. I really said that to myself. Dating was really getting very tiring. The first person I thought of was Michelle who still lived in Danbury. My friend Bob and I ran in a road race in Danbury and I called Michelle to come over to Bob's apartment and hang with us after the race. I had known Michelle for multiple years before dating and we always got along so well without any drama. From that day we got back together, and it was forever. We got engaged four months later and married in August of 1992. The second-best decision I ever made after accepting Christ.

As I have mentioned Michelle is from Jamaica and is a woman of color. She is also younger than me but is extremely mature and very stable. Despite our age difference she is more mature and stable then I am. Later in the book I will talk a lot more about my wife and my family. Only God can put a girl from Jamaica and a lily-white boy from Brookfield, CT together. I was so blessed to have her she is the best. I truly adore my wife.

Career

My career did not start off with a bang. I worked with various companies after I left Perkin Elmer and it made me wonder if I made the right choice. Should I have gone to law school should I have gone into finance. Most of my jobs were coding and troubleshooting application systems. Sitting at a desk all day in front of a screen was not really stoking the creative fires. I was bored and really wanted out, I needed to have a job where I could be around people and not look at a screen all day.

My break came when the father of a girl I dated worked at IBM and submitted my resume within a new division in the company called Professional Services. Here is God again in my life. The interview could not have gone better. Len, the person who interviewed and hired me became a great friend and I know God put him in my life.

We worked on my first project together and he really showed me the ropes within IBM. You will not find a more class act than Len, very funny and he is incredibly loyal friend. When we talk or see each other it is like we have been apart only days, not years. I owed my getting hired and my early career knowledge to Len.

The most important person in my IBM career and my IBM best friend was Cheryl. No doubt God put her in my life to mentor me. I think Cheryl thought I was raised by wolves. I know I was older now but not having anyone early in life take the time to teach me some basics saw me lacking in certain areas that other guys my age already have mastered. Most of the time she was cool about my lacking's but there were times she would let me have it. We enjoyed each other's company as friends, but she was my boss and she never showed favoritism with me. In fact, she was probably harder on me then other people who worked for her. Cheryl wants you to think she is this tough Italian girl from Buffalo but even though she does not suffer fools well she had a heart of gold. Cheryl and I are still friends today.

I was doing consulting and project management type work and it really fit me like a glove. I loved the work and project management was revered as a skill in IBM. In the later years everyone thought they could do it by passing some lame test. In my mind it dumbed down the profession. That was a real shame because it is a skillful job which has been basically turned into babysitting.

At first, I worked in New York City, Westchester County, Poughkeepsie and New Jersey region. I lived in New Fairfield, CT so the commute was not great but was manageable. On my projects in Poughkeepsie, we hired a lot of contractors to code on the application that we were developing. In the area was the Culinary Institute of America where they trained the great chefs. The salespeople for these contractors would take us there for the most amazing lunches. After eating I just wanted to go back to my office, shut the door and sleep.

Our organization was reorganizing so I was offered the opportunity to work out of the Hartford branch. I took the offer and so did my friend Cheryl, so it was on to the Hartford branch. I bought a townhouse in Farmington, CT. I really liked the town. My home was very near to Tunxis Community College and ESPN was right down the road in neighboring Bristol. I always ran into ESPN guys around town and in the airport. Stuart Scott and I liked the same pizza place in Farmington, nice guy. I loved Talcott Mountain and the West Hartford Reservoir for hiking and running. I really got into hiking I even hiked up Mt Washington in New Hampshire with a close friend.

I lived there for ten years from 1990 to 2000, I got married while I lived there and brought home my daughter Paige and son Kyle. We went to a great church there and made a lot of friends. Taking backroads, I could get to Litchfield County area quickly from Farmington. My sister lived near Lake Waramaug in New Preston and I would run around the lake which was about 7 miles around. On one of my runs, I shared the road with James Taylor. He was riding his bike and was nice enough not to run me over. I bet he did not have a 26-inch Schwinn bike.

My sister was nice enough to let us have our wedding reception under a tent in her backyard. We had the ceremony in an old Congregational Church with the traditional steeple. My wife also talked me into having a harpist play during our wedding reception. I must have really been in love. I am not a big wedding guy. I don't mind going to the ceremony it is the reception that is too much for me.

I have been fortunate to travel all over the world and the USA and I am truly amazed at the beauty of the State of Connecticut. Today, I live in North Carolina. It is a large state with access to the Ocean, the Outer Banks and the Mountains. The drawback is they are all hours away from my home. Being a smaller state, Connecticut allowed you to take in its rolling hills and the ocean within an easy drive. You can quickly get to the states of Massachusetts, Rhode Island, New York, Vermont, New Hampshire, Maine and Pennsylvania within hours. I love all the little towns which each have their own special character. If it was not for winter and the high cost to live there, I would really consider a move back to New England.

IBM Hartford

Moving to Farmington was also good for my career. IBM was just getting into the services market of the computer industry. IBM's main revenue had been hardware, so this new division was not as valued by the hardware branch of the company. The term *"I sold a lot of iron in my day"* seemed to be the mantra of the hardware reps. IBM was a leader in this market and had a huge market share so selling hardware was the driving force. This hardware services revenue split would have a dramatic change in years to come. The computer industry went to distributed processing with smaller machines having the same CPU power as the big boxes. In the mid 1990's IBM had to redefine its business model to become a more software and services company.

At the start, we were the stepchildren of IBM, they even put us on our own floor to hide us from their customers. The excellent part was our division bonded together. With few exceptions our team of about two dozen people all got along really great. We were all around the same age. It was kind of like an extension of college and we hung out socially and had a lot of fun together.

Ann Marie was the ringleader and social director. I used to tease her about it but in reality, we were all very thankful for her activity planning. Since I was single when I first arrived it was a great introduction to the area. Though lower Connecticut and the Hartford area are in the same state to me they seemed worlds apart. Lower Connecticut was really a suburb of New York City and Hartford area was more like New England. The easy way to break it down was lower CT rooted for the Yankees and mid CT rooted for the Red Sox. I am still in touch with most of them today. Good people, we really got along greatly.

The office was right across the street from the Hartford Civic Center and I would go to hockey games, UCONN basketball games and concerts. There were times at the end of the day I would walk out of the office and buy a single ticket to an event from someone who had an extra ticket. A few years into our marriage, my wife started working in downtown Hartford so we would go to lunch and visit each other. My friends were happier to see her then they were to see me. She became part of the group.

I had found my niche as a project manager and I was good at it. My contracts were with the State Government, United Technologies, Insurance Industry and I was asked to implement a whole new computer system for the City of Danbury. Working with the City of Danbury was a bit weird and nice since I grew up in that area. I would run into old friends and a lot of guys that I umpired in the Brookfield Baseball Association. At lunch a lot of times I would get a sandwich and eat by the Lake Candlewood. I got to know every person in city government. Local politics can really be rough.

The City of Danbury computer shop was unionized so they did not do anything that was not in their job description and I mean anything. We had just installed very expensive computer equipment when the air conditioning was faulty causing significant water damage to the floor. When I walked in, I asked if anyone called maintenance, they said no it was not their job. Despite potential damage to the computers, they were in the risk of being electrocuted. So, I ran upstairs and demanded to see either the city planner or the mayor. I was rebuffed until I explained the dire nature of the situation and we finally got it taken care of. I shook my head for days thinking about how absurd these people were. There are other examples of this apathy but that would be another book.

Soon I was offered to project manage a World-Wide Analytic database. Michelle and I did not have children at the time, so I took this job which led to a pretty good promotion. I got to travel all over the world and spent a lot of time in Australia and England. I loved this job and I met some people though this project that are my friends today. I actually traveled around the world. New York to London and then London to Sydney then Sydney to the San Francisco back to New York. I loved London and the British countryside. I still want to be British when I grow up. My mom's maiden name was Trefry and her roots are said to be in Cornwall. If I ever had the opportunity to live in the Cotswolds or the coast of England, I would seriously consider it.

Overall though my favorite city is Bruges in Belgium, it has great canals and it is just a cool small city with the best chocolate and French fries ever. The Belgian people were so very friendly, and the city was so easy to get around.

When my friend Keith was going into the service, we drove from Florida to Houston Texas in the summer in a car with no air conditioning. Each city from Mobile to New Orleans to Biloxi was hotter than the previous. I thought I would never feel that kind off heat again until I walked out of the airport in Bangkok Thailand. I was in a suit so in the matter of minutes I was pure sweat. It is the hottest and most humid place ever. I was never so uncomfortable; it was just so hot.

A good friend I met on this project was an Irish English native, Chris. Chris was a warrior; she was fearless, and I think that came with her having once been very close to deaths door and survived cancer. Chris and my wife got along great and we hung out together when the project had meetings in both New York and London. Chris lived in London and would show me around the area and all the best spots. We were in a department store in London looking for a gift for my wife when I realized that the actor, Alan Rickman, was standing next to me at the checkout counter. I said to Chris, *"Look, it's Hans Gruber we need to get out of here!"* I was referring to his bad guy character in the movie Die Hard. Mr. Rickman, smiled and nodded at us so I think we were ok. I think he was one of the greatest villains in motion picture history.

I loved running all over both Sydney and London going around their famous landmarks. Since it was hard to come home for the weekend, I explored whichever country I was in a lot and just really loved it. After running I went into a local market in London to get some water and a bite to eat. There was a big commotion in the store, and I asked the cashier what was going on. It seems I walked right past Margaret Thatcher as I entered the store. She was no longer the prime minister at the time she was just doing a little shopping. I never really noticed her.

On one run, near the Tower Bridge, some boys were playing soccer and the ball got in my running path. I kicked the ball over to them and they said thanks and I said you're welcome. They realized I was an American, and you would have thought I was a rock star. They asked me a ton of questions and asked me to play soccer with them and I did for a couple of hours. A great afternoon was had by all. My experiences overseas have led me to believe that Americans are generally well liked in most countries. I never ever had any issue in my travels, people seemed helpful and always wanted to help me enjoy their hometown. When I was in the suburbs of England, France, or Belgium, I was treated with the utmost respect.

I loved going to zoos as I traveled for IBM. In each city I would visit a zoo and spend hours there hanging with the animals. My favorite zoo is in Sydney which had animals that I was not accustomed to seeing. My favorite animal is the Giraffe, when I get to heaven, I am going to ask God what he was thinking when he created this animal. What is it? Of the ten most deadly snakes in the world nine of them reside in Australia so if you are in the woods in Australia be careful.

Another thing about Australia I liked was at night you saw totally different stars since we were in the Southern hemisphere. The seasons were in reverse as well while we experienced winter, they are experiencing summer. I loved visiting Australia; I just did not like at all the nearly twenty hours in the plane from Hartford CT. The worst was smelling the breakfast service after my routine of taking two Tylenol PMs to help me sleep on the plane. Waking up to the smell of fake eggs was brutal. On the long flights I had to get up and walk around the plane to avoid leg cramps.

After the database was designed, I was offered a position in Raleigh, NC to continue the projects effort. I moved to a suburb of Raleigh called Cary in the spring of 2000. We now had a two-year-old and a six-month-old. Like marriage I was a little late to fatherhood, but I had no regrets I loved being a father, even though I was previously uncertain about fatherhood because of my background. Once kids were in the picture, I vowed to be the best parent I could possibly be. My initiation into parenthood is a miracle in itself and it proved that God wanted the best for me.

IBM became a company in major transition both with the definition of the company and the way it treated its employee base. When I was first hired, I thought I hit the lottery. Respect for the Individual was the motto of the company and as long as you did your job you would have full employment. That disintegrated in the 90s when IBM started to lose market share and the stock dropped to an all-time low.

Massive layoffs, cost cutting, selling of real estate all in an effort to reduce cost that led to a dramatic change also to the human aspect of the company. You were now a number not a person and once they went down that road the cost cutting and layoffs became a continued process. Employees were now in survival mode and it did not lead to team chemistry which a project manager needs to survive.

With kids and a new challenge facing my family I decided to take a career-stifling job and work internally with IBM corporate office instead of customer focused service team. I disliked working in this group, but I needed to be home more, and I wanted to be a part of my kids growing up. I missed my customers, but the constant travel was really hard on my family. This new group was a far cry from cohesive unit I was used to working with and I felt my creativity was checked. I was a fish out of water in this group and I am not fond of office politics.

I was committed to putting my family first, so I stayed in this group for ten years and we accomplished a lot as a team, but it really didn't matter. I received good performance reviews for my work until I hit the age of fifty-five. Suddenly, I was deemed not a great performer. They were looking to cut me for a cheaper global resource. I had every indication that they were writing up a negative performance review on me and they did. I began hoping to get laid off and eventually I was two years later while working in another IBM organization. I accepted the nice severance package and retired from IBM. Financially, I had planned well, I knew this day was would come. The corporate game had changed for IBM and other companies.

I owe a lot to IBM, I had a great source of income, I traveled to places all around the United States and the globe and I retired with a pension. They paid for me to relocate to Cary, North Carolina an area I love. I gained a lot of skills that help me today in my everyday life. I developed public speaking skills in this job and still enjoy getting in front of an audience. Though the company focus change over the years, I still look at the good times and life experiences that were overall a blessing.

I took another consulting job for a few years, but I no longer had the heart for it. I was tired of having all the responsibility but none of the control and recognition for my successes. As companies engaged cheaper resources globally, project managers really became paper pushers and babysitters. I decided to leave the field since I also had to deal with my sons' illness at the same time. My project management career was now over and didn't regret my decision.

Now that I was no longer working, the years of on-the-job stress, incredibly long hours and uncertain employment took a significant toll on me. I now had free time and instead of enjoying it, I began to feel anxious about not working and our finances. Which really was not an issue. I did not handle this time well and really neglected my signs of mental decline. I went from full throttle to basically looking for things to do. I did not plan well for this new phase of life.

Dad's Death

When your father passes away, it is a big event. You will remember the date, year and how he passed. You may cry thinking of the good times or even be angry if there were not many good times. My father passed away in 2015, around the very time I stepped back from my job. I found out when my brother texted me on my cell phone. I still find that odd that he didn't call me, he just sent a text. For me it was, sadly, a nonevent. I wasn't terribly moved by the news. There were no fond memories of him nor was I cursing his death.

I found it sad, because no one in the world really cared that he died. His wife had died a year or two earlier. He never maintained a relationship with his brothers or their kids. It was a bizarre experience. My siblings talked about getting together at some point to reminisce about his life and spread his ashes. That was not going to happen because in reality, what in the world could we talk about that was positive and I did not want to go to a bitter fest. I had long made my peace with who he was and had forgiven him, he had no control or significance in my life other than by biology he was my father.

At the end of his life, my father was angry with me because he thought I received too much inheritance from my stepmother, and he wanted the money back. He was actually angry, embarrassed and humiliated over the fact that his wife left me more money than she left him from her estate. So, my dad refused to talk with me.

The last thing he did on this earth was to write me out of his will. It had no effect on me at all, nothing my father did mattered to me anymore. I actually felt so sorry for him. This man with all the talent in the world died without anyone caring or loving him. There was no obituary, no funeral, no ceremony just a bunch of ashes that sit in an urn in my brother's house.

In the process of writing this book, for the first time ever, all my thoughts and feelings were laid out on paper in regard to my father. It may seem that I am hard on my dad for his actions and lack of actions. In fact, it may seem I hold bitterness toward him. I truly have forgiven him and have released my pain to the Lord. I believe we make choices and those choices often affect others. The real sadness was that he was blind to how his actions affected his family. Maybe he just didn't care, I honestly do not know which it was, not caring or blindness.

While he was alive, I was respectful to him, helped him when he needed a hand and not once made a derogatory comment about him to my kids. I am proud that my kids saw that I was nothing but kind to my dad and drove to Hendersonville frequently to see how he was. I am not angry or bitter with my dad and God has blessed me with a tremendous family of my own.

Overall, I feel nothing but sadness for my father so much talent seemed to be wasted on his desire to be someone special but that seemed to exist only in his mind. The experience of what I went through made me double my efforts in being the best husband and dad to my family. I never wanted my kids to feel like I did, not even for one day. Though I made mistakes I would also acknowledge my errors and resolve issues with my kids. If the past did not happen to me. I might not have had that desire for my family that I have today.

Deeper Manifestations

After I left the work environment I had more free time and my level of anxiety and depression rose and was really off the charts. I wanted help but I was ashamed. I believed that as a Christian I should live by Philippians 4:6-7 and 13. I should not worry and live like I can do all things through Christ who strengthens me. Great verses and they have inspired me in my life but at this time I was ill. Those verses were not taking away what I was experiencing in fact they made me feel more guilty.

At times I would hear preachers discuss these verses and make it sound like you did not have enough faith if you struggle with these mental disorders. I know that they were trying to be encouraging but I really needed medical help.   Trust me I wanted more than anything to snap out of it but that was not going to happen. I love the Lord with all my heart and I knew what the bible said that we can be overcomers by the word of God but this was not one of those times. I truly needed help and God would provide it.

Pastors and other Christians, I implore you not to be judgmental when you encounter people who really have struggled with these issues. I know what the bible says about anxiety and worry but getting through these things is just not that easy. I was sick and needed medical care. In my readings I have discovered that some of the greatest Christian heroes such as Charles Spurgeon, Martin Luther and Mother Theresa documented their struggles with anxiety and depression. It didn't make them look weak, hopeless or rejected by Christ and they were not alone in their struggle.

What you say and how you act can play a big part in someone's recovery. People who are suffering do not need a spiritual giant, they truly need compassion love and understanding. Remember we are servants of God and his mercies are new every morning. Also, we have a soul, but we also have a body that his susceptible to pain. We are promised no pain and no tears only when we get to heaven our glorious destination.

The brain is an organ in our bodies so why would it not be susceptible to sickness. Even though I knew this and read a lot about the things going on in my life I still would not accept these things happening to me. I can get through this, I thought. I was very stubborn, and I was very wrong. Please get help if you are feeling anxious or depressed. I might have avoided what was about to happen to me if I gave in to my pride.

Again, my heart goes out to anyone who has to watch someone go through either Dementia or Alzheimer's. Watching my stepmom was not at all a pleasant experience, she would hallucinate, become easily agitated and not really know who we were. There are many great resources available on the subject of treating, slowing and even preventing Alzheimer's Disease. I found the book End of Alzheimer's by Dale Bredesen quite helpful and informative. The author encourages the use of vitamins, diet and good sleeping habits to ward off cognitive decline. I found it encouraging that we can take proactive steps to help in battling dementia type diseases.

Most humans have felt anxious, depressed or out of control at some time in their lives. Jesus who was both God and human sweated droplets of blood as he prayed the night before his crucifixion. Knowing what was ahead of him caused anxiety within him. He asked the Father to, *"take this cup"* from him. He was overwhelmed with sorrow but submitted to his father's will. Still Jesus was focused on his mission which we will discuss further.

I have seen a lot of struggling with mental issues; my mother, my stepbrother, my son would battle anorexia and my stepmother with Alzheimer's. All were devastating and all were no one's fault. I should have been more alert to the signs that I would succumb to my own mental health battle. I was truly a ticking time bomb. I would have bouts of anxiety and depression, but I would recover and think I just went through a phase. I would eventually suffer a break down and I would need some drastic measures to get back.

My son, Kyle is a great kid, but he is like my mom very sensitive and does not understand why anyone would be cruel and hurtful. Pretty sad that someone so sweet has to struggle in this social media self-serving world we live in. Kyle is very handsome; he stands at 6' 4" and he has a heart bigger than he is tall. I never ever heard a person say anything but good things about him. While playing football he suffered a major concussion that really set him back in his high school education and since he was not a strong student anyway it had its devastating implications. He had to work really hard to graduate. What was natural for most kids was a major achievement for him.

While he was nursing his concussion at home Kyle put on a lot of weight and was teased when he went back to school. He did not tell us what had been happening. We have since learned that he endured severe bullying. He developed anorexia and lost over 100 pounds in a few months. We recognized it as he was progressing from just eating salads to eating less and less. Nothing we said or did changed it. He was determined to keep going until he lost all the weight he wanted. When we said, *"that's enough"*, he'd say, *"not enough yet"*. It was a frightening battle for all of us. Anorexia had complete control of this boy. The more we insisted, the more determined he became about not eating. Anorexia takes hold of the mind with a fierce grip. It can be a long battle. We were finally able to get him into in-patient treatment.

Checking him in to the treatment facility, that day was very hard. I was deep into my illness. Anxiety and depression were in control of me. I was losing my son. It was a battle for me to be mentally present during the meeting with the admitting staff to sign papers and make payments. I was unable to comfort my wife who was completely broken.

He had never been away from home for more than a night's sleepover with friends. We were placing our child into the hands of people we didn't know. The facility was highly recommended, it was modern and cheerfully decorated to accommodate young people. But we were still terrified of what he would go through. He would undergo several medical tests, have individual and group therapy, food preparation and art classes. From the outside, it seemed like a camp. We knew that a lot of hard work was going on there.

We saw young people at various stages of eating disorder. It was gut wrenching watching beautiful teens and young adults struggle with anorexia some had to be force fed with feeding tubes. The parents in our discussion groups poured out their hearts with stories of multiple years these diseases had impacted their family unit. I was proud of Kyle because he was well respected and was looked up to by the other patients. He is still in contact today with some of those friends he made.

Kyle didn't want to have a feeding tube inserted so he complied with meal requirements as much as possible. The facility requires family involvement in the treatment process. There were educational opportunities for the family each week. I didn't make it to most of those things. I was admitted soon after he was for my own treatment. Kyle was in treatment for five months; half of that time was out-patient but still intense daily sessions. It was an extremely busy time for the family. There was a lot of running from place to place.

Coming to a Head

Not dealing with my past, the work stress I was under, hormone imbalance, trying a number of different prescription drugs and my sons' condition, and intense guilt all collided, and I was severely depressed. I was overrun by anxious, dark thoughts, fear, deep depression. I cried out to God, but he seemed so far away, I felt that God had forsaken me and that he hated me and wanted me to suffer. Most of all, I feared that another family member in my life was going to be destroyed by mental illness. Could God be so distant and not caring?

During one of my earlier bouts with depression I began taking an antidepressant. It worked well and I just stayed on it for years. At some point it was no longer effective. During all the stresses with my job, I was exhibiting more signs of not coping well. I would ruminate nonstop about the lies and unfair circumstances. I played things over and over in my head. I would easily become aggravated with people for behaviors that I really should have been able to let go. My doctor changed my medication and we had a few changes over a few months. Some of these medicines elicit the same symptoms they are intended to relieve. So, the first weeks on a new drug could see a person experiencing more intense anxiety or depression. Things just spiraled. I was getting worse and no one had an answer for why. Psychotherapy did nothing to help. I went from therapist to therapist, doctor to doctor and nothing worked.

It is impossible for me to express the dark place I was in and the mental anguish I suffered. I have torn my knee, pulled my hamstring, had two root canals and have broken my nose 12 times. None of those alone or together at once can compare to the pain I felt during this time. I could not sleep; I was lethargic and really had no emotions whatsoever. You are trapped within yourself and the world around exists in blackened hollow space. I was a shell of myself surviving each day praying and hoping it would end. My joy was completely gone, and my maturity reverted back that of a child.

I had a lot of difficulties going out in public. During this time. I would shake violently and feel like the walls were collapsing all around me. On one occasion, I took my daughter on a college visit during her senior year in high school. I honestly do not know how I survived, it was just brutal, and I am surprised I did not just collapse. A big moment in my daughter's life and I was shaken but no matter how hard and painful it was I wanted to be part of her life, so as best as I could I continued my duties as a father. I hid these feelings from my daughter as best I could, she never mentioned it to me. Each time this happened I felt incredible shame.

Was I suicidal? Honestly no, but I really thought that my family might be a lot better off without me. So, if I died, they could go on with their lives and not have me troubling them. I could not be more wrong. I know if I had died it would have devastated my family and today, I am so grateful for life and see it as a true gift. I thank God every day I am alive, and I never take that for granted.

Finally, in a hopeless, helpless state, I was hospitalized. I didn't want my wife and kids to go through what my siblings and I endured. My diagnosis was medication-resistant depression. Beside the depression I was very upset with myself that I did not fight this on my own. I cannot express enough how ashamed I was.

Duke Hospital

Duke University Hospital's psychiatry clinic specializes in electroconvulsive therapy (ECT). This was a scary proposition, but we were desperate for help and relief from this pain. ECT is an approved medical treatment that involves using electricity to produce a brief seizure in a person under general anesthesia. My treatments began during my hospitalization. After about 10 treatments with very little improvement the medical team determined that I required higher intensity treatments. After a few more treatments of higher intensity stimulation, I began to improve. I was able to leave the hospital after two months and continued with a few out-patient treatments.

ECT, for lack of a better term, a wild process. Prior to the start of the procedure, I had to have an intravenous port placed in my arm. That could take a while for me since you had to be hooked up to the right vein. Once that was completed, I was put in a wheelchair and travelled for what seemed forever to the part of the hospital where ECT was being performed. That trip alone to the ECT lab caused severe anxiety and stress. It felt similar to Fairfield Hills with the long eerie hallways.

Once there I am strapped to a table with multiple electrodes placed on my legs and both arms. I had wires on every inch of my body checking for heart and any other vital signs. Lastly a helmet like apparatus is placed on my head with more wires coming out in multiple directions. The setup took a good fifteen minutes before I was sedated for the procedure. Since I was unconscious, I didn't feel the jolt to my brain.

Overall, I felt I was in Young Frankenstein with Gene Wilder, Teri Garr and Marty Feldman looking over me screaming *"It's Alive"*. I was then going to get up and tap dance with Gene to Putting on the Ritz. You had to see the movie. In about twenty minutes I would wake up in their recovery room, they conducted a few brief tests to make sure I was fine and that ended the overall ECT. Not something I really planned on happening in my life. It showed my level of desperation.

During my hospital stay, I was at the lowest point of my life and I remember crying out to God. Why am I going through this? One morning while crying out, I felt a sudden sense of peace. I heard a voice saying, "*I will never leave you, nor forsake you*". I know it was God's Spirit speaking to my inner man. From that day forward I had hope. Within days the decision was made to increase the intensity of my ECT treatment, and I began to improve and shortly I went home for good.

Antidepressants and psychotherapy can ease depression symptoms for most people. But these are not enough with medication-resistant or treatment-resistant depression. When I think back to the various psychiatrists and therapists I saw during my suffering, I shake my head. They were well meaning, but no one identified that this deep depression would not improve with just medication or therapy. My experience with therapists did not leave me with a warm feeling.

I won't paint all therapists with a broad brush. My criticism is not aimed at the entire profession. I must believe that there are many highly effective therapists in practice today. My unfortunate case is hopefully not the typical experience of most patients. I saw so many therapists over the course of about 2 years that I have lost count. I do remember that there was one who spoke mostly of himself during the sessions and one whose opinion was that my fear and anxiety were sin.

That leads me to think the best practitioner is one who has personal experience with these mental health issues. I think there would be a higher awareness among these practitioners. Nevertheless, there are therapists who have broad clinical experiences that help them to effectively treat patients. The other helpful discovery in my health care is an integrative medicine doctor. The physician works to treat the whole person rather than just the disease.

During my illness, I was still Dad and I tried my best to continue in that role by maintaining my interactions with the kids. At the worst part of my illness, my daughter was finishing up high school and the chaos continued into her freshman year of college. I took her on college tours, and some trips were a real battle as my anxiety and depression were relentless. She had her dream role in the school's spring production. There was prom, graduation, college orientation and dorm move-in day. I was physically present for everything, but as hard as I tried, I was mentally absent. I was suffering terribly.

As I mentioned before, at one point both Kyle and I were hospitalized at the same time. So now I talk about the real hero of the family and that is my wife, Michelle. I cannot imagine what she went through, I know she cried herself to sleep many nights. She questioned and argued with God about what was happening to her family, the one thing that she cherished above everything. Paige really stepped up and helped her mom while she was finishing up her senior year. With everything she had to accomplish to graduate, she was able to take on additional family responsibilities and provide the support her mother needed. Paige never complained once. She stepped up graciously to the tasks that needed to be done. I was so proud of her and still am today.

Earlier I discussed how hard it was for me to visit my mother in a psychiatric hospital. Looking back, I understand what my wife had to go through during this time. The man she loved, who was the confident leader of the family who protected her and the kids was now a shell of himself. Visiting Kyle and me in various hospitals, knowing we had to stay in these facilities until we were well, must have just crushed her spirit. The big question was, would we both recover from these mental illnesses? I know that she felt very alone. She never gave up on me she knew that while I was sick that this was not me. She never stopped seeing Kurt and not just the severely depressed and lost person.

My wife's love and belief in me was unconditional, I owe her a debt that I can never repay. She hates when I say that she feels that what she did was natural. I know the marriage vows we spoke on our wedding day, but she went beyond and she was a major part of our family being the tight knit unit we are today. Our family endured the proverbial trial by fire and it only made us stronger. Michelle, Paige, and Kyle are the main reason I thank God every day I am alive just to spend another day with them. I do not fear death I just have too much to accomplish on earth before I am in glory with my heavenly father. I want a lot more of life.

We are thankful for the friends and family who provided support to our family at this time. The brother in-law who accompanied us to appointments, the neighbors who mowed our lawn, the pastor's wife who spoke with Michelle regularly, her bosses who allowed her flexibility to take care of her family's needs, the list goes on.

We learned a lot about how to support people we know during difficult times. What we've learned is that when someone is hurting, or in need of support, some people step forward and most stay away. Don't say, *"Let me know if you need anything."* My advice is to take a look at what they are managing, what they are struggling to keep up with or just think of something kind to do for them without asking. Send them a gift card for a meal, grocery or gas. Many people hold back when others are going through difficulties. I guess they feel they would be intruding if they reached out.

Nobody has all the answers or always knows the right things to say, that is not your job as a friend or family member. Your job is to care and help-out even without being asked. Be there to listen while they talk. Hold them up when they are too weak. Please do not ignore a situation when you can help.

When my son talks about that dark time in our family, he rightfully says his mother is the strongest person he knows, and she deserves all the accolades. I know I put her through a lot during my sickness, I leaned on her like a child, I wanted her to help take the pain away. Obviously, she was not able to do that. I know I was annoying. I know she realizes that I was very sick. Writing this made me realize how much I have taken her for granted and I hope not to make this mistake again. I adore my wife and I am a very blessed man.

Spiritual Battle

For our struggle is not against flesh and blood,
but against the rulers, against the authorities,
against the powers of this dark world and against
the spiritual forces of evil in the heavenly realms.
Ephesians 6:12

If anything, I learned during my illness that the verse above is very true and also very real. While I was sick the evil one, Satan, without question played havoc with my thought life. During this time, I continually battled thoughts that I was not saved or loved by God. I felt hopeless, worthless, helpless and I was constantly sad. Sometimes I was devoid of any emotions neither sad or happy.

Wild thoughts that I would never ever entertain in the past were being fed into my mind. I was in an extreme spiritual battle. I was a walking zombie and the continued barrage from Satan was relentless. Looking back this may have been my most difficult battle. During that time, I was not Kurt Yanik at all, but God and my wife would not give up on me. The mental pain was exhausting and it drained me physically.

I had grown into a pretty confident person who knew what I was good at and what I was not good at. I had fought through so many things all my life. Why would God allow this to happen, what did I do that was so wrong? Seriously, how much more did he expect me to take? Why do my wife and kids have to suffer? I asked, *"why God?"* over and over.

All you have to do is look in the bible and see that multiple people suffered through various emotional battles. Job had his whole life turned upside down, David in multiple Psalms expressed severe stress and fear. The prophet Elijah became depressed. I am in no way equating myself to these biblical giants but what we all had in common is at the end of the day we knew where our help came from and we trusted him. I never turned my back on God, and he never turned his back on me.

I started to recognize my family and friends' love for me and my faith was starting to be restored. Even while I was in the hospital, I would pray for people and talk about Jesus and I know that God saw my compassion for my fellow patients. Despite my situation I still loved people and would constantly talk to both patients and the staff.

Today, I understand Satan's tricks and do my best not to let him get to me. It is something I definitely learned during my trial. Our Lord's love is so much bigger than anything that Satan can throw at us and if we really understand that then we will be ok. Someday Satan's head will be crushed and there will be no room for him in God's paradise. We defeat Satan by the blood of Jesus.

I Feared Losing Myself

My biggest fear during that time was losing myself, my joy, my goofiness my passion for life. Was I going to be stuck with this cloud of depression over my head? Will I still be a good father and good husband? Can I have joy in church again praising God and reading his word? Would I do the family finances again? Go back to work in any capacity either part time or full time. Could I be in the moment Would I root for the New York Giants again?

What would bring back my passion, my love of life, being thankful and experiencing joy again? Would I smile again? Would my eyes sparkle and laugh and giggle like I used to? Would I try to make people laugh (my favorite hobby)? Would I see good in the world, in my family, in my life?

All these thoughts and shame were going through my head as I was getting ready to go home. I so wanted to go home but I was very apprehensive and probably a bit scared. The love of my family neighbors and friends would alleviate all my doubts.

Even when I knew I would come out of it I was concerned of the residual affects this would have on my health and my interactions. I just wanted to be Kurt again, I feel so good when I am just Kurt and truly all I ever wanted was to get back to him. It seemed simple but the road was full of doubts but God had other plans for me. I would never be just the old Kurt again. God made me the new and improved Kurt. He molded me through this battle into the person he wanted me to be and I am still working out the kinks.

Coming Home

I was very happy to be home from the hospital; I would never feel anxious or depressed again but I now felt totally ashamed. For weeks I avoided seeing people or speaking with anyone who called. I spent a lot of time in my den away from everyone. Since I was continuing with ECT on an out-patient basis, I was dealing with short-term memory loss and guilt as I was trying to resettle myself at home. The healing process took about two years from 2016 to 2018 but it was a lifetime in coming.

I was ashamed because I felt I let my family down, for a period of time my kids and my wife did not have me. I was around but I was not me, not dad. I was mad that I allowed this to happen, I had fought all my life as an underdog overcoming some of the most horrific things a person can go through but this just got the best of me. The first weeks at home turned to months during which time I really did not do much but eat, sleep, do bible devotions and walk the dog. I wasn't depressed. I just needed to come back to myself.

My dog Pepe really helped me through my shame and loneliness, my dog never left my side. Every day I would take him to the dog park or we would go for a walk. He made me get out of the house and that was so necessary. I was truly amazed by how my dog seemed to sense and react to my moods. When I was down, he would come over and put his chin on my leg. He still does that to this day. I am a true convert to the whole dog people thing.

I was concerned about how people would receive me after being away. Would they see me as some nut case who could not handle his emotions? A person who left his family for a while and just couldn't handle life. I definitely hid out a bit because of that. Through my devotions and prayer time I realize God was with me all the time. He allowed me to go through this pain, but he was in control all along. I am a control freak and with my background a lot of times I had to make my own way. God had another plan for me he wanted all of me and I had to relinquish control. When I did that, and God used the experience to make me a better and more caring person.

I was blessed that my neighbors; friends and my church family received me back like nothing happened. There was no judging just love and that was a big healing moment for me. I was Kurt before, and I was Kurt again. An older woman at church came to me and said that it brought her joy to see me again smiling and it gave her hope as she dealt with her own issues. I cannot express in terms what this support meant to me, not one time did anyone approach me in trepidation or look at me uncomfortably.

During coffee with my friend Pete, I asked him what he thought of me and my suffering. He told me that I was an inspiration to him and how I stayed loyal to my faith and he did not judge me. I came very close to crying and I changed the subject quickly to avoid crying in front of him. The healing continued and it did not take that long to be back, not to just Kurt but a more improved Kurt redeemed by my savior Jesus.

I thought I had to reconcile with my wife and my kids. I tried to say that I was sorry, but they would have none of that. They were just so happy I was back and basically better. I had nothing to apologize for, they understood I was sick, and I needed to get better. I am so thankful that I was in a financial position that I did not have to go back to a highly demanding job. I was able to spend time with my kids and help my wife while she worked. I believe I was where God wanted me to be.

I became a substitute teacher. I worked mostly in my son's high school. It was close to home and Kyle was going through his own readjustment period as he went back to school after completing treatment. The flexible schedule allowed me more time with him. It warmed my heart that he was always happy to see me when we would run into each other in the halls at school. Kyle would later tell me that my being around for him during his healing was a great aid to his recovery. That was a blessing to be there for my sweet boy. That time together helped to create a very strong bond between the two of us. We love the NY Giants, UCONN, the Beatles but most of all, we love the Lord. Thinking back, maybe if I did not get sick and continued to work crazy hours, I would not have been there for him. Remember God works out all things for those that are called and love him.

My daughter was at college about an hour and a half away, so I often went down to take her to lunch or dinner. She always brought along a friend and we enjoyed the time together. My wife and I would never miss her jazz performances and I really enjoyed the music. My kids had their dad back and we never discussed my illness. I thought I had my family back but in reality, I never lost them. I was still Dad and that is a form of love that I am so blessed to have in my life.

My relationship with God strengthened as he lifted me out of the pit and started to mold me into what he wanted me to be. For the second time I felt that I heard God speak to my inner man. I knew he was telling me that I would never go through that mental anguish again. I was set Free, what a gift from the creator of the world. Today when I feel any anxiety, I rebuke it in the name of Jesus and to be totally honest I am done with suffering for a bit. Satan has been defeated by Jesus and he will have no place in the heavenly realms which is a Christian's true home.

A real special gift from God was that I have very little memory of what I went through in those two years of suffering. Even some everyday events have slipped my mind. I realized this when I was watching a Captain America movie at home and told Kyle to come in and watch it with me. He looked at me puzzled and told me I had already seen this movie. It turns out, he and I went to the movie during our own struggle. I honestly had no memory of it. I realized that there are many details during my suffering that I do not remember.

My wife has since told me that some church friends drove me to some of my treatments and I had no recollection of that ever happening. My kids have even mentioned that I took them places that I do not remember. Those events I missed but I am glad that I am able to not recall many of the traumatizing things I had to endure. I believe that not remembering details of the worst times is evidence of God's protective nature toward me. An amazing blessing, I cannot thank God enough. God healed my mind from some very unpleasant events.

God's Blessing, My Family

Proverbs 31:10
An excellent wife who can find? She is far more
precious than jewels.

I got married on August 8, 1992 to the rock of our family. Michelle is elegant, beautiful, loving, caring and she takes our marriage and motherhood very seriously. Her family is the most important thing to her on this earth. She wants nothing but the best for me and the kids and will sacrifice for our goals. I never met a person more loyal and giving than she. Bottom line Michelle Yanik is the best person I have ever met in my life. I have learned so much from her and I need to even kill my stubborn nature and listen more. Michelle is a major blessing and though I do fail I really try to be the best husband that I can be.

The biggest key to our relationship is we are honest with each other and I hid nothing from her, and she hides nothing from me. I stated upfront that my wife will not be surprised by anything in this book and she has read it and has given me the ok before it is published. Michelle, like myself had to deal with some things in her past and she has handled them with extreme dignity. I waited a while to get married. God gave me the best friend, lover and partner. My God is a God of blessing and this one was my best.

The next step was being part of an extended family. I probably have not always been fair to my extended family and it really stems to how uncomfortable I am around families. It is something I still deal with today, a lot of people in a room with all these personalities and noise can really weigh on me. I do not have a big family, but my wife does, and they can be overwhelming at times. It is my flaw and I need God to help me with it. I have gotten better at it but need more work in this area.

I was not pushing for us to have kids at first but once it happened, I got on board, I made a pledge that I would not let them feel like I did for one day. I made mistakes at times, but I have the two best kids in the world. Even at my age they still want to hang out with me, and never make me feel they don't want me around.

My daughter Paige is the most determined person in the world. She graduated with a degree in music therapy in May 2020. Unfortunately, that was during the Covid-19 Pandemic lockdown. Her major requires a six-month internship following graduation and then the diploma would be granted. Due to the lockdown Paige would not be able to start her internship as planned. She was already working with clients of the Autism Society and took on a second job with a similar company providing services to people with physical or mental disabilities.

Almost a year later, she was finally able to begin her internship and completed it while working with multiple clients. I admire her work ethic and drive. She is such a joy, and still hugs me before she goes to bed every night. She is doing what she loves, helping people to achieve goals and push through their adversities. It is a joy to watch my first born become a lady.

She is moving out of the house soon and will be sharing an apartment with a college friend. Though she is close to us in Raleigh, I will still miss her a lot and so will my dog Pepe, that dog adores Paige. In fact, if anyone tries to hug Paige, he barks at them in a jealous fit.

Our son Kyle was born in 1999. The kids are 18 months apart. My heart is overjoyed that they get along together so well and look out for each other. Kyle is very athletic and has a huge heart and is universally loved by anyone who comes into his path. I am so proud of the man he is becoming, and we share the same love for the New York Giants. Both kids follow Christ and for that I am most grateful.

Kyle is mechanically inclined as well; he puts all the items together that we buy that need assembly. He does not really read instructions; he naturally can put things together. He has saved me a lot of frustration because I am the worst person in the world at assembling anything. I have broken more things than I have actually built.

Adversity will either destroy you or bring you closer together with the people that matter. Today Kyle is doing very well. He is taking college classes and getting grades that I think even shock him. He is working at a great job and I think I see a career path for him and like all of us he is a work in progress. I see improvement in him every day and he is knocking out his issues every day.

I gave them five simple rules which I hope they will continue to live with:

1. Never walk away from your relationship with Christ
2. Stay away from Drugs and Alcohol
3. Marry a God-fearing person
4. Be kind and generous
5. Stay out of debt

We do have one other family member that I can't overlook, our dog Pepe. I never bought into the animal lover theories until I got this dog. He is a weird mix of a Dachshund and Labrador and it is beyond cute. He really cracks me up. There is no doubt he is my dog because he follows my every move. We love going to the dog park and for rides in the car. I've mentioned how he stuck by my side when I returned home. Even today when I walk out the door, he stares at me as if he's wondering if I am going to come back.

One of the most interesting things about my marriage is that my wife is from Jamaica. On my visit there it is a beautiful country, but it is a third world country with goats and cattle walking on roads. I went on a run up a hill near my wife's grandparents' house. As I ran back down the hill a man with a huge machete came out of the woods. I thought I was a dead man, but the man was farming in the woods and he kept his crops in check with the machete by pruning and cutting the vegetation. He knew my wife's grandparents and walked with me back to their house and we talk for a bit. No way that weapon is sold in the USA.

Overall, Michelle, Paige and Kyle are so important to me and we do have an incredible bond among us. I care so much to do the right thing for them. Beside pleasing God, they are my main focus. I want people to like me and I do not feel I ever give anyone a reason not to like me, but I really care about those three the most.

Since I am semi-retired my wife Michelle is the consistent bread winner of the family and she has been blessed with a job that she loves. She is very good at her job and is a great asset to her department. Though it is sometimes demanding she has a great work life balance and is still able to give attention to home and family as she loves to do.

My wife does not have a selfish bone in her body and her immediate family comes first in every way. She is more serious than I am, and she can be seen rolling her eyes at some of my goofiness. We are a blessed family and have become through it all a very tight knit group.

Contentment and Direction

Lamentations 3:22-23
22 The steadfast love of the Lord never ceases;[a]
his mercies never come to an end;
23 they are new every morning;
great is your faithfulness.

The Lord has called me to repent and hold no grudges. I hope that people have also forgiven me for offenses of which I may not even be aware. God has forgiven me of my past, and he ask us not to dwell on it but to learn from it.

Above all in my life, I have learned to be content in all my situations in life. Certainly, I like the good stuff so much more than the bad stuff. It is Christ spirit within me that got me through the pain and agony of life. It is a way to have peace knowing that whatever position I am in life it is going to be ok in Jesus Christ.

Not that I am speaking of being in need, for I have learned in whatever situation I am to be content. I know how to be brought low, and I know how to abound. In any and every circumstance, I have learned the secret of facing plenty and hunger, abundance and need.
Philippians 4 11-12

I started the book off with Romans 8:28 which states, and we know **all things** God works for the good of those who love him, who have been called according for his purposes. The person I am today is because I am a work in progress molded by God and **all things** he works out for his benefit. That includes the good the bad and the ugly. Jesus Christ is Lord and I would like to introduce him to you, if you did not already know him.

I am a better person today not because of what I did but what God did through me. I am blessed to know Jesus Christ and he has been by my side through it all. My wife Michelle has a lot to do with making me a better person, it is so important to have a mate who is on the same page spiritually as you. My kids also make my life full of contentment. When things got really rough, I never heard them complain, they both acted with a level of maturity beyond their years. What really matters and what really kept us was our faith and trust in Jesus Christ. He kept my family together during a time of strife and grief and today we are an incredibly close family.

THANK YOU, JESUS.

Prayer of Thankfulness

Lord I am totally amazed by how you worked and continue to work behind the scenes in my life. Your timing may not have been when I wanted things to happen, but your timing is always perfect. Thank you for setting me free from my past. Thank you for saving me and calling me your own.

For you are the Lord of Lords, King of Kings, Savior, Abba Father and my friend. You are able to do exceedingly, abundantly more than we could ever ask or imagine.

Why we Suffer

Suffering stinks. It is even worse when we watch someone we love suffer. It is especially painful when we see our children suffer. Did you know that most of Jesus' disciples suffered immeasurably and died horrific deaths? We live in a fallen world and pain is going to happen. It is inevitable, we all will suffer and it sucks.

Suffering can make us better people. That sounds so odd but it is true. I learned more out of my pain than I did during my moments of glory. Our experiences enable us to help others when they suffer. Through suffering we can be molded into the person that God wants us to be if we yield to his authority and allow him to mold us. I can honestly say that my faith, compassion and my ability to love have increased with my adversity. Adversity has many effects on humans.

I can appreciate another person's pain and truly empathize. I am not mad at God for my suffering, I am actually thankful. As thankful as I am, I really do not want to repeat some of the things I went through. Once was enough and my human capacity is at its limit. I do believe God has given me mercy and grace in that area. I have been to the top of the mountain and in the pig sty but in both cases, God was with me. He never left me.

Paul, a disciple of Christ sums up the real reason we suffer in the verses in 2 Corinthians verses 3 through 7.

3 Praise be to the God and Father of our Lord Jesus Christ, the Father of compassion and the God of all comfort, 4 who comforts us in all our troubles, so that we can comfort those in any trouble with the comfort we ourselves receive from God. 5 For just as we share abundantly in the sufferings of Christ, so also our comfort abounds through Christ. 6 If we are distressed, it is for your comfort and salvation; if we are comforted, it is for your comfort, which produces in you patient endurance of the same sufferings we suffer. 7 And our hope for you is firm, because we know that just as you share in our sufferings, so also you share in our comfort.

It is an example we all should follow. We are on this earth to be servants and to work with and help those who are in need. The greatest servant of all time was Jesus Christ the son of God.

Grace Revisited

9 But he said to me, "My grace is sufficient for you, for my power is made perfect in weakness." Therefore, I will boast all the more gladly about my weaknesses, so that Christ's power may rest on me. 10 That is why, for Christ's sake, I delight in weaknesses, in insults, in hardships, in persecutions, in difficulties. For when I am weak, then I am strong. 2 Corinthians 12:9-10

Paul was suffering with a great ailment and he asked God three times to take it away, the bible is not specific about what the ailment is but it bothered Paul enough that he pleaded with God to remove it. What God gave Paul was a lesson in grace and that though we will have pain, issues and sorrows our Lord Jesus can get us through them.

In reading this book, please understand that the only reason I survived my tribulations was by God's grace and love for me. Even when I was not serving Christ even when I would sin against him and use his name in vain, he never stopped loving me and looking out for me. We live in a fallen world where there is death, sickness and pain. No one is immune, we all go through times of being in the valley and we have to deal with it.

I am alive and very blessed, and I am not kidding when I say I am the most blessed man on the planet. Through my relationship with Christ, I have learned to be content in all matters.

Prayer Through difficult times

Lord through your word helps us to be content in all matters. It does not mean we have to like what is happening to us but that we must go through things to strengthen us and to truly understand that you are with us even in the valley of the shadow of death. Lord this may be the hardest thing we will pray for but let us have knowledge that you may not necessarily be angry with us but that have something so much better for us as we go through each and very battle.

Destiny with Death

This title sounds like one of those old B level horror flicks or a short story from Edgar Alan Poe. Though the title seems a bit morbid it is my hope that I gained your attention. At my age I have definitely lived more years than I have left on this earth. I must face the fact that inevitable I and you are going to die and end this time on earth. Since we are going to die, we must assume that this earth will not be our final resting place nor was it meant to be.

Death is not a fun topic to discuss especially when it is a person taken at a very early age. Some of us will die young and some of us will have a longer time on this earth. Overall, our lifespans are a blip on the radar screen compared to eternity.

We may have all experienced shocking deaths at some point, maybe someone we loved was taken from us at an early age. Apart from my experiences in my family, I remember vividly the untimely deaths of President Kennedy, John Lennon, Princess Diana and just recently, basketball player, Kobe Bryant. Each death took the world by surprise. They were victims of murder or an accident within a vehicle. The world mourned these lives for weeks. Though we were dismayed at the early age we lost these people, we cannot be alarmed that they died because we all will die. It is just a matter of time.

The well-known song *Turn, Turn, Turn* by 1960's band The Byrds' repeated lyrics straight from the scriptures.

> *"There is a time for everything,*
> *and a season for every activity under the*
> *heavens:2 a time to be born and a time to die,..."*
> *Ecclesiastes 3 1-2*

We plan for so many things in our lives, we plan for financial security, our kid's colleges and retirement. We may plan for our death with a will and getting a cemetery plot but are we planning for eternity? Where will we exist after our physical body gives out?

Jesus, when talking to his disciples made them a promise in the verse below. At the time, the disciples were not in a good state and Jesus comforted them with this verse.

> *"Let not your heart be troubled; you believe in*
> *God, believe also in Me. In My Father's house are*
> *many mansions; if it were not so, I would have*
> *told you. I go to prepare a place for you. And if I*
> *go and prepare a place for you, I will come again*
> *and receive you to Myself; that where I am, there*
> *you may be also." John 14: 1-3*

The Bible describes over 7,000 promises of God throughout its chapters. When God makes a promise to his people, it will come to pass. What is a promise? A promise is a covenant or declaration that one will do exactly what they say or an event that will happen just as pledged. I cannot even count all the promises that I have broken to people but God breaks none of his to me or you.

Good news

God created this world and everything in it. His plan was to have fellowship with man. Sin entered the world through Adam and Eve's disobedience. Sin separates us from God. None of us could ever be good enough to be worthy in God's sight. God provided a way back to fellowship with him through the sacrifice of his one and only son. Jesus is the only perfect, sinless one. He suffered and died in our place. He took all the sins of the world on himself. He paid the price for our sins that we could not pay. He died, and was resurrected giving us the hope of a resurrected life. All we have to do is believe in Jesus and repent of our sins and we will gain eternal life with him.

For all have sinned and fall short of the glory of God Romans 3:23

As it is written: "None is righteous, no, not one Romans 6:10

We are all sinners and in God's eyes everyone is in the same boat because of our sin nature. No class system, no income levels, no celebrity status to God we are all his children every one of us.

To God all sin is disobedience and to the human mind that is tough to grasp. God hates sin but he loves us and he wants us to recognize our sin and deal with it.

Do not feel alone, some of the great Bible heroes committed some real whoppers when it came to sin but they experienced God's love and forgiving nature.

- Paul, the great evangelist was a persecutor of Christians before he encountered Christ and became an unwavering servant of God.
- King David committed adultery and murder, yet he was said to have had a heart after God.
- Moses committed murder and disobeyed God but continued fellowship with God while leading his people in the wilderness.
- Peter, out of fear denied knowing Jesus three times but he repented and led the first church.
- Abraham lied about his wife to protect himself. Yet God fulfilled his promise to make him a great nation.
- Noah got drunk and disgraced himself and his family, yet he is still notable for his faith and obedience to God.

And just as it is appointed for man to die once, and after that comes judgment, so Christ, having been offered once to bear the sins of many, will appear a second time, not to deal with sin but to save those who are eagerly waiting for him.
Hebrews 9:27-28

All mankind will one day stand before a holy God. The question is, do you want to stand before him knowing that your sins have been forgiven by Jesus or do you want to take your chances in arrogance. I assure you; it will be a terrifying experience to stand before the Almighty God of the universe. I believe even those of us who are assured of our salvation, will quake in our boots in his presence.

The prophet Isaiah, after describing his vision of God, high and exalted, seated on a throne, recognized his sinful state and how unworthy he was to be in God's presence.

> *"Woe to me! I cried. "I am ruined! For I am a man of unclean lips, and I live among a people of unclean lips, and my eyes have seen the king, the Lord Almighty." Isaiah 6:5*

What is our response to the Good News? Believe and receive.

> *If you declare with your mouth, "Jesus is Lord," and believe in your heart that God raised him from the dead, you will be saved. 10 For it is with your heart that you believe and are justified, and it is with your mouth that you profess your faith and are saved. Romans 10:9-10*

The scripture above is God's greatest promise to you and it is free of charge. It is the greatest gift to mankind and it is better than any earthly possession you might crave. You give nothing but yourself and you gain so much more both on earth and in heaven. What's so great on this earth that keeps us from letting go and letting God rule in your heart? Is it pride, sinful desires, status or possessions? This world is coming to an end. In Matthew 24, Jesus tells us just that, and tells us the signs that will indicate the end.

> "4 Jesus answered: "Watch out that no one deceives you. 5 For many will come in my name, claiming, 'I am the Messiah,' and will deceive many. 6 You will hear of wars and rumors of wars, but see to it that you are not alarmed. Such things must happen, but the end is still to come. 7 Nation will rise against nation, and kingdom against kingdom. There will be famines and earthquakes in various places. 8 All these are the beginning of birth pains." Matthew 24:4-8

Some of these things are apparent in our world today. We are living in a world that is in serious self-destruct mode. The solution is to give your heart to Christ and become a new creation in him. The world will oppose you but you will be welcomed into the kingdom of God by his son Jesus. That is why we call him savior; he saves us from what we deserve because of our sin and gives us freedom.

God loved us so much that he allowed a human access to Heaven through visions. In the book of Revelation John, a disciple of Christ, spells out basically the wonder of salvation and judgement on a world which turned its back on him. If you remember John was the one disciple who witnessed the crucifixion of Jesus and was a great comfort to Jesus' mother during that time. I can see why he was chosen to get the glimpse of heaven. What an honor.

Then I saw a new heaven and a new earth, for the first heaven and the first earth had passed away, and the sea was no more. And I saw the holy city, new Jerusalem, coming down out of heaven from God, prepared as a bride adorned for her husband. And I heard a loud voice from the throne saying, "Behold, the dwelling place of God is with man. He will dwell with them, and they will be his people, and God himself will be with them as their God. He will wipe away every tear from their eyes, and death shall be no more, neither shall there be mourning, nor crying, nor __pain__ anymore, for the former things have passed away." And he who was seated on the throne said, "Behold, I am making all things new." Also, he said, "Write this down, for these words are trustworthy and true." Revelation 21:1-5

No more pain only joy, peace, worship, jubilation and utter thankfulness. I have a lot still to do on earth so I hope and pray the Lord gives me more time here, but heaven is perfection. Just like our savior is Perfect. Just think of your best day on earth and multiply it by infinity. That is what heaven will be like.

Let me say this, hell is a real place. It is a place of eternal separation from God. In the absence of God there is no peace, no joy, no light. Imagine an eternity in spiritual and physical darkness. We are mystified by some of the evil humans can inflict on others. Imagine living among the most evil beings and being subjected to their cruelty day after day, without end. Hell is full of the most vile creatures. Satan only want to bring along as many of us as he can. He wants man to believe that he isn't real, hell isn't real. The fact is, hell is real, Satan is real and we must choose where we will spend eternity.

Please ask Jesus to reveal himself to you and take the next step and allow him to work in your heart. All your problems will not vanish, but a peace and comfort will come over you and it will be the best high you will ever encounter. On a daily basis he is my comforter, gives me peace of mind even in stressful times. He is my counselor providing advice, he is my helper for relief and support. He is my advocate and he strengthens me each day in my effort to finish the race we are all on. He intercedes and prays for me and gives me peace. Let him do that for you.

Servitude

Above all the ways we describe Jesus, he was God's servant and was obedient to his calling. In my walk that is the one thing that sticks out to me is being a servant. Jesus was God but he still wanted to serve mankind despite all our corrupt ways.

Philippians 2 verses 5 through 8 describes his humility perfectly.

In your relationships with one another, have the same mindset as Christ Jesus:

6 Who, being in very nature[a] God,
*   did not consider equality with God something*
to be used to his own advantage;
7 rather, he made himself nothing
*   by taking the very nature[b] of a servant,*
*   being made in human likeness.*
8 And being found in appearance as a man,
*   he humbled himself*
*   by becoming obedient to death—*
*   even death on a cross!*

The last night prior to Jesus' crucifixion he fed the disciples and washed their feet. Who does this but God? Jesus knew he was to die but he is washing twelve pairs of stinky smelly feet. Imagine for one second, Jesus the King of Kings and Lord or Lords was humble enough to wash the feet of the people who were his followers. There is no example of humility that I can think of that can compare to this. Jesus who is God never used his position as a power grab he just served.

Jesus as the verse points out was obedient to death, he did exactly what his father intended. He never took advantage of his position, and he was God. If Jesus was called to serve, what does he expect from us. Serving is both caring and doing and it is for all to participate in. Serving should be with no strings attached but if we expect something in return, we are just making a trade of good deeds.

Without any remorse I have really learned that serving others brings about contentment, joy and peace. I truly believe giving is better than receiving and that even means giving to people who may not deserve it. Jesus died for my sins and I did not deserve this gift, but it was freely given.

Blessed Life

I would not leave you with the impression that I have had an absolutely awful life. I am a very blessed person who had some pretty lousy things happen to me. I am a child of Christ and thankful for every breath I take. Each morning I wake up I thank God that I am alive to tackle the day with joy and excitement. My countenance has changed dramatically, and I do not have that look of anguish on my face anymore. I am in my sixties now and I feel like I am in my thirties. I smile constantly and I just enjoy the smallest things. I am so happy to be alive and I want the lord to give me more years to accomplish things he has set before me.

God also had to deal with me when it came to my temper. I needed to really just put aside my desire to have things my way and when I want them. Anger often comes from the misconception of one's own importance. I have definitely toned it down quite a bit but still have my moments. I'm a better listener and which leads to better communication.

Going through all that I have been through has helped me gain perspective in difficult situations. When issues arise today, I think through them and I ask God for guidance. By drawing closer to Jesus, we learn to trust him. John 15: 4-5 below gives us every hope for us to have success with Jesus Christ in our lives.

Remain in me, as I also remain in you. No branch
can bear fruit by itself; it must remain in the vine.
Neither can you bear fruit unless you remain in
me. "I am the vine; you are the branches. If you
remain in me and I in you, you will bear much
fruit; apart from me you can do nothing."

Since God is creator of the world, don't you think he can help you with your issues and show you the love that you so desire? No major direction or problem goes without prayer, and I am very thankful even if the answer does not always line up the way we think it should. Even when I may veer off the path, Jesus doesn't throw me overboard and point his finger at me shaming me. He is our advocate with the father, and he wants the best for us but overall, he wants us to be part of his kingdom and that is a choice we have in our power to make.

1 John 1:9
If we confess our sins, he is faithful and just and
will forgive us our sins and purify us from all
unrighteousness.

Jesus wants to talk to you and that is the main reason he created man. He wants fellowship with his creation, and he totally cares about you, your family, and your life. Overall, we will decide whether or not to have a relationship with God and you will be called at some point to decide. The decision is an individual one that is yours alone. Jesus cares about all that you deal with and he wants you in his kingdom.

Every morning, for the most part, I get up read my bible and pray giving time and thanks to our lord. It sets the day off correctly. I am not perfect and make a lot of mistakes, but I try to fix them and move forward. I want to see my kids get married and have their own kids if it is God's will for them. I am a very blessed man and I am very thankful for all my blessings.

Today, I feel like I have recaptured that little boy in Darien who just loved life and all it has to offer. Following Christ and knowing that the creator of the universe knows my name, loves me, and truly is in control of all things, gives me assurance each day of my life. I am so thankful for the peace that I have that is truly beyond my understanding.

Gods Blessings for you

I loved writing this book even though it reminded me of things that were in no way pleasant. Like I said earlier this is really the first time I have shared my story so a lot of my friends and family members will be surprised by what they read. I am a relatively private person, so I did have to overcome that aspect to write this book. Once I got started, the information poured out of me effortlessly and I believe I was inspired to tell my story because of my relationship with Christ and the love and support of my amazing family. I have been very open with my story and I hope I helped you to realize that we all have our trials. Most of all I hope I opened your eyes to my Jesus and if you don't know him, I hope you will want to know him.

If you are suffering from any mental disease, I implore you to get help. Ask for God's direction and seek proper medical treatment. Research and pray for direction in choosing the right doctors, the right therapy and the right care for you.

Do not feel ashamed because you are struggling, it happens to a lot of people and you need to reprimand anybody that tells you to just get over it. There is no shame in asking for help, I wish I got help earlier and had not been so stubborn or headstrong. I wish I knew to deal with my trauma rather than suppress it.

You have my total sympathy in this challenge you are facing, and I beg you not to give up because God has a purpose for your life. No matter how low you feel one day you will rise out of this pit of despair, if I can do it so can you.

It would be odd for me to thank God for some of the events in my life. It would seem weird to be grateful for all that happened to my family but as a result of or in spite of all that trauma I can recognize God's love and provision for me. I have an understanding of things that only come from going through trials and in that sense, I am very blessed.

Today, I am still a goofball, I am 65 going on 14. I am a husband, a father, most of all I am a child of the most-high God. Jesus was not just a nice guy, not just the greatest human to walk the face of the earth, not just a prophet, but Jesus is the King of Kings, Lord of Lords and our Savior. Jesus is God. I hope to meet some of you in heaven. Together we can have fellowship, praise our Lord and tell of his goodness to us.

I would like to end with five great blessings for you and your family. God totally loves you. Thanks for reading my book and please let God bless you. It is up to you; he is always there and waiting.

May the LORD bless you and keep you; the LORD makes his face to shine upon you and be gracious to you; the LORD lift you up his countenance upon you and give you peace. **Numbers 6:24–26**

And the peace of God, which transcends all understanding, will guard your hearts and your minds in Christ Jesus. **Philippians 4:7**

Now to him who is able to do immeasurably more than all we ask or imagine, according to his power that is at work within us, to him be glory in the church and in Christ Jesus throughout all generations, for ever and ever! Amen. **Ephesians 4 20-21**

May you experience the love of Christ, though it is so great you will never fully understand it, and may you be filled with the fullness of life and power that comes from God. **Ephesians 3:16,**

May God be gracious to you and bless you and make His face shine upon you **Psalm 67:1**

Final Thoughts

I hope my story has been helpful and somewhat inspirational to you but please do not be inspired by what I did. The inspiration is what Jesus did through me. Looking back and reflecting I really started to think of the joyous times I had growing up even in the Dark Decade. What I experienced with the dark events and what I had to endure were rough, but I still had and have great friends, experiences, adventures and overall, a very blessed life.

One of the highlights for me in writing this book was that I had great thoughts and a sense of real peace when thinking about my mother. My mother was a fantastic person who just got very sick, died way too young and that was a real shame and I do miss her. Mom influenced me when it came to my decision making as I grew older and her voice in my head helped me in my healing process. It really was a relief to think of her as the person she was and not the suicidal ending. She had beautiful blue eyes and the most amazing smile, and I miss her enthusiasm. Mom was just a lot of fun to be around and a bit of a goofball like me.

If you are reading this book and I may have acted irrationally towards you or hurt you, I am truly sorry. I was never ever my intention; my mind just went in so many directions and I was trying to make it through each day. Everyone who has been part of my life is part of this book and I am grateful to you in both the good and the bad. Everything I went through was just a voyage that we just call life.

I never wanted pity, nor wanted to be a victim. Most of all I was adamant about not letting these challenges define me and I learned two very valuable lessons.

1. Iron sharpens iron and I have been through multiple fires and though I am very far from perfect, I am spotless in God's eyes through the blood of Jesus. I also want to make sure you understand that I am not better, smarter, or more together than you. I am saved totally by the grace and mercy of God. this a blessing that is available from every person of every race. Bottom line I was and am a sinner who needed and still needs my savior, Jesus Christ. In the book of Romans, the Bible is quite clear on God sees all of us

2. Love does conquer all, simple and sappy but true.

   Love is patient, love is kind. It does not envy, it does not boast, it is not proud. It is not rude, it is not self-seeking, it is not easily angered, it keeps no record of wrongs. Love does not delight in evil but rejoices with the truth. 1 Corinthians 13:4

The verse above is powerful and really takes a Christ like attitude to put in motion. I have learned over time to just be nice and caring looking at each person as special in God's eyes. As we go through our day, we encounter people who are going through all kinds of things. Wouldn't it be nice to smile and talk kindly to them, you never know whose day you can make.

It is my hope that God grants me his favor and that this book will reach and encourage a wide audience. I awake each day thanking God that I am alive and I see life as a gift. I have had great days in my life but I always think tomorrow will be better than today.

Life can be challenging and complicated but there is so many things we take for granted like each breath we take, a sunrise, laughter, people who love us, the ability to walk, leaves changing in the fall, a smile, our homes and a real good chicken salad sandwich. Be content and grateful there is someone out there who has it a lot worse than us and they may do nothing more than just smile. Lastly, God always has and always will bless us with **Sufficient Grace**.

I would like to hear your thoughts. Please email me at *sufficientgrace752@gmail.com*.

In Christ

Kurt Alan Yanik

Acknowledgements

I would like to thank the people who helped to make this book possible.

A special thank you to my friend Luann who, having written several books, was first to encourage me to begin writing this book.

During the process, I had multiple streams of input and editing. I am especially grateful to my in-laws Kirk and Milly, friends Cheryl, Rose and Dana for their valuable contributions.

Lastly, all would be naught if my family had not been there with daily encouragement.